POLICE
PROBLEM SOLVING

QUINT C. THURMAN
Texas State University – San Marcos

J.D. JAMIESON
Texas State University – San Marcos

Police Problem Solving

Copyright © 2004
Matthew Bender & Company, Inc., a member of the LexisNexis Group

Phone 877-374-2919
Web Site www.lexisnexis.com/anderson/criminaljustice

LexisNexis and the Knowledge Burst logo are trademarks of Reed Elsevier Properties, Inc.
Anderson Publishing is a registered trademark of Anderson Publishing, a member of the LexisNexis Group

Police problem solving / [compiled by] Quint T. Thurman, J.D. Jamieson
    p. cm.
    Includes bibliographical references and index.
    ISBN 1-58360-536-3 (softbound : alk. paper)

Cover design by Tin Box Studio, Inc.

EDITOR Elisabeth Roszmann Ebben
ACQUISITIONS EDITOR Michael C. Braswell

Acknowledgments

The initial idea for this book arose during conversations with LeRoy Broner of the Federal Law Enforcement Training Center (FLETC) in Glynco, Georgia, as well as with others at the National Center for State and Local Law Enforcement Training, including Malcolm Adams. They deserve the appreciation of our entire nation for their recognition of the need for the law enforcement community to work beyond traditional responses to crime and related problems. Simultaneously, our sincere acknowledgement goes to our nation's public safety practitioners who proudly wear the uniform and solve problems every day.

Contributing authors to this book come from a wide variety of backgrounds. As experts in their disciplines, they bring to this work a rich array of perspectives and innovative examples of successful problem-solving initiatives. We feel extremely fortunate that they chose to share their insights in this book.

Finally, we wish to extend our thanks to Elisabeth "Biz" Ebben, Academic Publications Editor at Anderson/LexisNexis and to our graduate assistant, Vicki Quintana. It was indeed a pleasure to work once again with Biz; Vicki, too, made this an enjoyable project and one that she can be proud of having worked hard to see to completion.

Contents

Section I

Introduction

Chapter 1

Introduction to Police Problem Solving

Steve Rutzebeck & Quint C. Thurman

Introduction

The complexity of modern policing requires the adoption of a problem-solving approach to public safety, as opposed to a more traditional, incident-driven orientation. Even so, policing from its very beginning has been a profession based upon solving problems. A typical police officer's day, probably more than a day in any other profession, is composed of a series of problems he or she is asked or required to solve. Thus, being effective as a police officer depends on the ability to effectively solve problems. And while many problems that arise daily demand immediate solutions and split-second responses, others allow time for thought and coordinated responses. This chapter offers a review of the principal approaches to problem solving in use by contemporary law enforcement agencies.

Background

Truly exceptional officers have the ability to see the big picture beyond the incident they face at any given moment. A talent for recognizing the community problem or problems that precipitated an immediate problem comes naturally to only a select few. For others, gaining this larger perspective is an ability and talent that has to be learned. The process starts with establishing an ingrained and structured approach in which to analyze the problem and arrive at the best solution. Accordingly, several different problem-solving models have been developed in order to guide the problem-solving process. This chapter offers synopses of some of the best-known problem-solving models currently in use by law enforcement.

Problem-Solving Approaches

SARA. SARA (Scanning, Analysis, Response, Assessment) is a problem-solving model first put in practice by the Newport News, Virginia, police department in the early 1980s by police officers and researchers working with the Police Executive Research Forum (PERF). Using this model as a springboard, many derivatives have been created. Each of these derivatives was developed as a response to a particular community need or as a way of promoting acceptance of formalized problem solving.

> **Scanning**—The identification of a cluster of similar, related, or recurring incidents through a preliminary review of information, and the selection of this crime/disorder problem among competing priorities for future examination.

> **Analysis**—The use of several sources of information to determine why a problem is occurring, who is responsible, who is affected, where the problem is located, when it occurs, and what form the problem takes. Analysis requires identifying patterns that explain the conditions that facilitate the crime or disorder problem. Sources of information may include police data (CAD, arrest incident data, etc.); victim and offender interviews; environmental surveys; officer, business, and resident surveys; social service and other government agency data; and insurance information.

> **Response**—The execution of a tailored set of actions that address the most important findings of the problem analysis phase and focus on at least two of the following: (1) preventing future occurrences by deflecting offenders; (2) protecting likely victims; or (3) making crime locations less conducive to problem behaviors. Responses are designed to have a long-term impact on the problem and do not require a commitment of police time and resources that is not sustainable over the long term.

> **Assessment**—The impact of the responses on the targeted crime/disorder problem using information collected from multiple sources, both before and after the responses have been implemented.

CAPRA. The CAPRA model was developed by the Royal Canadian Mounted Police (RCMP) in the early 1990s. Although the model has much in common with SARA, it adds two important components—Clients and Partnerships. The RCMP thought that these were so important that they needed to be identified separately by the problem solver when going through the problem-solving thought process. CAPRA emphasizes how one must work with clients to define and solve problems.

Clients—The RCMP defines clients as the people with whom police interact in the delivery of their services and the people for whom that service is delivered. All who have an interest in the services that are provided must be considered in order to ensure that their interests are taken into account regarding how services are delivered. The better their interests are understood, the more quickly and effectively their needs can be met, as well as their demands and expectations in terms of service delivery (defining problems, establishing priorities, deployment of personnel, assessing how service standards are met). Understanding a client better helps to dissipate potentially violent situations before they erupt. Having this understanding helps mobilize the community to assist in achieving safe homes and safe streets by solving community problems and generates workable and sustainable preventive actions. Two types of clients are identified: (1) *Direct clients* are those with whom an agency interacts at various points in service delivery or investigations; (2) *Indirect clients* are those not directly involved in an incident or its investigation but have an interest in its outcome either because of the way it was handled or because of the association of the incident to similar incidents.

Acquiring and Analyzing Information—This includes gathering information essential to the investigation or handling the investigation incident. Many police officers restrict their information gathering to the facts directly related to the specific incident or occurrence. The more comprehensive the information gathered, the better an agency is able to effectively analyze a problem.

Partnerships—Partnerships can include anyone within the organization, other government departments or agencies, or the community who can assist in providing better quality and timely service. Establishing and maintaining partnerships increases the amount of resources (i.e., manpower, finances, etc.) and solutions available for addressing a particular community problem. The more partners an agency engages, the more trust that is built for increasing the effectiveness of solutions and having a lasting effect. Partners might come from within a police department or community as well as externally (e.g., doctors, social workers, psychologists, scientists, lab technicians, canine specialists, fire fighters, clergy, and colleagues with experience or expertise in a particular area). Partners can be thought of as part of the problem-solving team, even if they may initially have been identified as agency adversaries.

Response—Response is about applying strategies to solve community problems. An agency that has done an effective job in the preceding parts of CAPRA will be able to develop appropriate response strategies that have a high probability of success. For every call for assistance or intervention, police have available to them four major types of response strategies: service, protection, enforcement, and prevention. Service is assisting the public and referring them to appropriate partners. Protection is defined as protecting the public, victims, and those affected by their victimization, in partnership with community agencies and experts. Enforcement entails enforcing laws through the judicial system so that offenders are held accountable. Finally, prevention involves preventing problems from occurring or escalating through intervention, proactive problem solving, and education. It must be remembered that there are usually multiple responses from which to choose. The skill is in choosing the option that results in the fewest number of negative consequences. There are six possible solutions to a problem: (1) totally eliminating a problem; (2) substantially reducing a problem; (3) reducing the harm created by the problem; (4) improving police responses to a problem; (5) redefining problem responsibilities; and (6) determining that a perceived problem is really not a problem after all.

Assessment—Assessment is the evaluation of the effectiveness of the response that has been chosen. The determination of what worked and what did not work is critical so that modification to the response or complete response changes can be made, if necessary. Ongoing monitoring of a situation is essential to the continuous improvement and success of present and future problem-solving efforts. Formalizing the assessment with written documentation allows for others to learn from your problem-solving efforts. It should be remembered that other officers are dealing day in and day out with the same problems and therefore there is much that can be learned from others' successes and failures.

SCAPRA. The problem-solving model SCAPRA evolved directly from CAPRA but with a slight addition. When the local Police Corps in Baltimore, Maryland, decided to write a problem-based curriculum for their academy in the mid-1990s, they decided on CAPRA for their problem-solving model but had one concern. They were afraid that police on the streets would not readily embrace the concept of problem solving because of their concern for officer safety. Problem solving and community policing were still viewed by many street officers as "touchy-feely" programs that did not reflect the realities of "real" policing. Recognizing this, the curriculum developers at Police Corps decided to address this issue head-on by adding another component to CAPRA—*safety*, hence the *S* in SCAPRA. The *S* signaled an acknowledgement that the officers needed to ensure their own safety as well as that of the community members they were interacting with. Assessing participant safety (officer and client) became a primary factor to determine before problem solving could continue. The safety issue was not just a front-end concern. Police Corps wanted to ensure that maintaining appropriate safety standards became part of the process throughout the problem-solving effort. Additionally, the term *safety* was not restricted to just immediate personal safety for the participants. The safety component also encompassed anticipating the reaction of the community to agency actions. Agencies need to think through how the decisions they make affect the future safety of other officers or community members.

SECAPRA. SECAPRA is a problem-solving model that resulted from an effort in the late 1990s by the Mid-Atlantic Regional Community Policing Institute (MARCPI), located at Johns Hopkins University, to develop a national problem-based entrance-level training academy curriculum. Again, as with SCAPRA, the foundation of the model rests with the RCMP's CAPRA model. MARCPI saw a need to add *ethics* as one more component to the model and so the *E* was added. This component required that agencies base their actions and decisions on good ethical principles—doing the right thing for the right reasons. Again, like safety, this was not just a front-end issue but an aspect that needed to permeate the entire process.

Fishbone or Ishikawa Diagram. The cause-and-effect diagram is the brainchild of Kaoru Ishikawa of the University of Tokyo, who pioneered quality management processes in the Kawasaki shipyards. In the process, Ishikawa became one of the founding fathers of modern management. The cause-and-effect diagram is used to explore all the potential or real causes (or inputs) that result in a single effect (or output). Causes are arranged according to their level of importance or detail, resulting in a depiction of relationships and hierarchy of events. This can help agencies to identify root causes, locate areas where there may be problems, and compare the relative importance of different causes. When complete, this technique looks like the skeleton of a fish. The primary purpose of this tool is to identify and list all the possible contributing factors of the problem at hand. The problem is written down and enclosed in a circle on the right side of the paper or whiteboard. A straight line is drawn to the left and appears as the backbone of the fish. The next step is to brainstorm all the possible contributing factors of the problem. These are displayed as stems off the backbone at 45-degree angles. To further break down the contributing factors, branches can be added to each stem.

This technique is most effective when employed over a series of meetings. In effect, it lets the subconscious "cook" the problem so that new ideas will come forth. Advantages of letting the process "cook" include the following: time for the subconscious to work on the problem, participants are less likely to be inhibited, as the authorship of a particular contribution will be forgotten and people may become more immersed in the problem if they think about it day and night.

The fishbone diagram is effective for many reasons. It encourages problem solvers to study all parts of a problem before making a decision. It helps show relationships between the contributing factors and the relative importance of those factors. It helps start the creative process because it focuses the problem solver on the problem. It helps start a logical sequence for solving a problem. It helps problem solvers see the total problem as opposed to focusing on a narrow part or symptoms only. It offers a way to reduce the scope of the problem and solve less complex issues rather than more complex issues. It helps keep people focused on the problem rather than going off on tangents.

Conclusion

These problem-solving models are just a few of those in use today in modern policing. Other problem-solving approaches that represent variations from those discussed in this chapter undoubtedly are being used. It is important for agencies to embrace some means to solve recurring crime and related problems in a logical and effective way rather than simply running from one call to another. Initially, agencies might even want to record their experiences as they go through the problem-solving process. A number of workbooks, which highlight the steps, have been published that can help in this process. As agencies become more comfortable with the process, the need for "written processing" may become less important or necessary. Effective problem solving is not just a policing tool, but a tool that is useful in many facets of life.

References

Cordner, G. (1999). *Community Policing: Principles and Elements*. Richmond: Eastern Kentucky University.

"Effective Policing Problem Solving Programs." (2004). Washington, DC: U.S. Department of Homeland Security, Federal Law Enforcement Training Center, Office of State and Local Law Enforcement Training, State and Local Programs Division.

Royal Canadian Mounted Police (1993). *Facilitators Guide to the RCMP Learning Maps*. CAPRA Problem Solving Model. Ottawa, Ontario: Author.

Southeastern Community Oriented Policing Education (1998). *Train the Trainer Manual*. Knoxville: University of Tennessee.

Thurman, Q.C., and J. Zhao (2004). *Contemporary Policing: Controversies, Challenges, and Solutions*. Los Angeles, CA: Roxbury Publishing Co.

Thurman, Q.C., and E.F. McGarrell (1997). *Community Policing in a Rural Setting*. Cincinnati, OH: Anderson Publishing Co.

Chapter 2

The Applicability of Police Problem Solving to Crime Problems*

Jeff Rojek

Introduction

Since 1993 the Police Executive Research Forum (PERF) has recognized successful problem-oriented policing initiatives through the presentation of the Herman Goldstein Award. Award-winning projects are those that provide innovative and effective strategies for reducing crime, and for disorder and public safety problems (PERF, 1999). The showcasing of these initiatives is meant to provide knowledge to other law enforcement agencies on best practices, as well as spur further innovation in the field. Consideration for the Goldstein Award is open to employees of law enforcement agencies worldwide who have engaged in the creation of problem-oriented policing initiatives (PERF, 1999). These individuals are required to submit a written proposal to the PERF award commission that provides a brief overview of the problem-oriented initiative, which must be presented in the SARA (scanning, analysis, response, and assessment) format (see Spelman and Eck, 1987; Goldstein, 1990; National Institute of Justice [NIJ], 2000). From 1993 to 1999 there were 53 problem-oriented initiatives recognized as winners or honor mentions by the award commission.[1] This chapter identifies the characteristics of these 53 innovative initiatives.

Background

The analysis of the initiatives was guided by two general research questions. The first was concerned with the nature of the problems addressed by the Goldstein nominees. As noted above, the request for proposals for the Goldstein Award sought initiatives that addressed crime, disorder, and/or public safety. The empirical literature on problem-oriented policing initiatives has shown a particular focus on crime-related problems (Matthews, 1990; Hope, 1994; Green, 1996; Braga et al., 1999; Mazerolle, Ready, Terrill, and Waring, 2000). In addition, recent analysis of the Problem-Solving Partnership grants provided by the Community Oriented Policing Services (COPS) office revealed that four of the five most commonly addressed problems were crime related (PERF, 2000).[2] The expectation of this study is that the majority of the Goldstein nominees have focused on crime-related issues. However, the model of problem-oriented policing established by Herman Goldstein (1979, 1990) has asserted that this effort should not focus on single crime or disorder problems. Rather, officers should identify the interconnected crime and problems in a given area that produce repetitive calls for service and demand for department resources in order to fashion a more comprehensive response. Thus, this analysis of the award-winning initiatives explored the degree to which officers identified interconnected problems as opposed to single issues.

The second question is related in the nature of response applied to the identified problems. Each of these initiatives is seen as presenting new ways of addressing persistent problems. A goal of the present analysis is to classify general response techniques. Examining these responses provides insight into the type of problem-oriented policing that is occurring. Eck (1993) has noted the existence of two models of problem-oriented policing—situational and enforcement. The *situational* approach represents the use of problem-oriented policing as a vehicle for creating innovative and diverse responses to problems, while the *enforcement* approach remolds the problem-oriented model in order to justify the continuation of traditional police practices. Since these initiatives are recognized as exemplary problem-oriented policing efforts, the expectation is that they will represent Eck's situational approach. In sum, the Goldstein Award nominees provide an opportunity to see what are the most commonly used techniques in successful problem-oriented initiatives and whether or not they are enforcement driven.

Problem-Solving Approach

The written proposals submitted to PERF by the 53 award-winning initiatives formed the basis for conducting this analysis. The problems and responses that were articulated by the officers and identified in each proposal were examined according to the two research questions. The characteristics of each of these were then categorized for their similarity to or difference from each other in order to provide some generalization across initiatives. In some cases the categorization was rather straightforward. For example, one proposal identified drug sales out of a specific house as one problem, and another identified drug sales taking place in a bar. In both of these cases, drug sales would be one of the classified problems for each initiative. On the other hand, the analysis required the construction of more abstract categories for techniques that were similar but differed in their specific application. For example, one agency improved lighting in a commercial area with persistent crime problems, and another altered sidewalk benches to inhibit drunken individuals from sleeping on them. Though each represents a specific approach to a different problem, both are representative of the common approach of crime prevention through environmental design (CPTED).

Results

Nature of the Problem

Consistent with Goldstein's (1990) premise, each of these initiatives addressed problems that produced repeat calls for service and the devotion of police resources. Also, consistent with Goldstein, 85 percent (n = 45) of the nominees had identified a number of crime and disorder problems associated with their problem-oriented policing initiative. To separate these numerous problems, the present analysis included a two-step process of problem identification. First, all of the crime and disorder problems indicated in each proposal were identified. Then the proposals were evaluated to determine if the officers were selecting one problem as being of primary interest over the others. This provided insight into whether they were identifying interconnected problems and if they were engaging in an analysis that identified the primary focus for resources that would have a greater impact on all associated problems.

In some cases the primary problem was clearly explained in the proposals. For example, in one initiative, prostitution, robbery, assault, and drug activity were identified as problems in a specific neighborhood. However, the officers argued that it was the prostitution activity that was the primary source for the development of other problems. The pimps followed the prostitutes into the area, which resulted in assaults between pimps and between the pimps and prostitutes. The prostitutes drew the "johns" in the area, which provided targets for robbery. Further, the introduction of crack cocaine among the prostitutes and pimps spawned the growth of drug activity. Based on this analysis, it was determined that prostitution was the primary problem that needed to be addressed.

In other proposals the nature of the problem required a more careful review. One agency had targeted the problems of drug activity, high crime, vandalism, and various other nuisances within a specific neighborhood. Drug activity was presented as a serious problem, but it was not clearly identified as the primary problem. Rather, the agency presented the problem they were addressing in a broader sense of a neighborhood with a concentration of crime and disorder. It was this later concept of a concentration of crime and disorder that then was identified as the primary problem. The validity of this classification was reinforced upon further evaluation of the response, which revealed a broader neighborhood approach rather than a focus on a specific element.

Table 1 illustrates the connection between primary and related problems. In the case of "Neighborhoods with Concentrations of Crime and Disorder" there are a number of other articulated problems. In eight of the nine initiatives that fell under this category, drug activity and high levels of Part I crimes were seen as important related problems. Further examination of Table 1 reveals that there was an identification of multiple related problems for 45 of 53 initiatives. It is important to recognize that the problems listed here are directed toward those issues that present problems for police officers in their everyday work environment. For example, in a neighborhood where drug activity is perceived as the primary problem, officers might also have to respond to related calls for service on gang activity, crime, and/or public intoxication. Additional negative consequences related to each of these initiatives exist but are not listed. These would include such factors as a loss in the quality of life for neighborhood residents, a decline in business activity, or a decrease in a sense of community. Unfortunately, there was a lack of consistency across the initiatives in specifying other community and social problem, which eliminated the possibility of evaluating these associated issues. Nonetheless, Table 1 demonstrates that the award-winning nominees operated in the spirit of the Goldstein model by identifying the interrelation between multiple problems that they and the community faced.

Table 1
Primary Problems and Related Problems Identified

Primary Problem	**Related Problems**
1. Neighborhoods with Concentrated Crime and Disorder (9)	Drug Activity (8) High Level of Part I Crimes (8) Gang Activity (5) Vandalism (5) Nuisance Activity (5) Transients (4) Problem Liquor Establishments (3) Abandoned Houses (3) Public Intoxication (2) Prostitution (2) Traffic Congestion

Table 1, *continued*

Primary Problem	Related Problems
2. Drug Activity (6)	High Level of Part I Crimes (4) Gang Activity (2) Public Intoxication (2) Truancy (2) Parole Violators Prostitution Problem Apartment Management Nuisance Activity Vandalism Transients
3. Specific High-Crime Locations (6)	Drug Activity (5) High Level of Part I Crimes (4) Gang Activity (3) Public Intoxication (2) Nuisance Activity (2) Vandalism (2) Problem Apartment Management Prostitution Child Abuse Child Pornography
4. Transient/Homeless Problems (4)	Theft (3) Aggressive Panhandling (3) Burglary (2) Drug Activity (2) Illegal Camping (2) Public Intoxication Nuisance Activity Vandalism
5. Prostitution (3)	High Level of Part I Crimes (3) Drug Activity (2) Vandalism (2) Problem Liquor Establishments Problem Motels Transients Lewd Acts in Public Gang Activity
6. Domestic Violence (3)	None
7. Gang Violence (2)	Drug Activity
8. 911 Hang-ups (2)	None
9. Problem Bars/Nightclubs (2)	High Level of Part I Crimes Drug Activity Nuisance Activity Vandalism Theft Prostitution
10. Truancy (2)	High Level of Part I Crimes (1) Drug Activity Vandalism

Table 1, *continued*

Primary Problem	Related Problems
11. Commercial Development	None
12. Juvenile Delinquency	Drug Activity High Level of Part I Crimes Vandalism Truancy
13. Civil Disturbance	High Level of Part I Crimes Vandalism Public Intoxication Traffic Accidents
14. Traffic Accidents	None
15. Lewd Conduct in Public	None
16. Excessive Use of Alcohol	High Level of Part I Crimes Public Intoxication Driving while Under the Influence Domestic Violence
17. Nuisance and Criminal Activity in Park	High Level of Part I Crime Drug Activity Public Intoxication Accidental Deaths Trespassing Nuisance Activity Traffic Congestion
18. School Disorder	High Level of Part I Crimes Trespassing Nuisance Activity Vandalism Traffic Congestion
19. Regulation of Group Homes	Assaults Nuisance Activity Vandalism
20. Drunk Driving	Accidental Deaths Traffic Accidents
21. Day Laborers	Assaults Drug Activity Public Intoxication Trespassing Nuisance Activity Gambling Traffic Congestion
22. Cruising	High Level of Part I Crimes Drug Activity Gang Activity Public Intoxication Nuisance Activity Vandalism
23. Fraud of the Elderly	Burglary
24. Child Custody Disputes	Court Order Violations

Nature of the Response

As noted above, another principal goal of problem-oriented policing is to address persistent problems, like those presented above, with innovative strategies. Table 2 presents 24 different strategies that were devised to resolve the primary and related problems identified by the nominees. Table 2 represents more than 250 responses applied over the 53 initiatives. Though each response was uniquely applied to the context of the problem in each initiative, treating each as unique in an analysis provides an impossible task for attempting to understand the current state of police innovation. Thus, the responses were grouped under similar approaches in order to illustrate a general sense of the innovative strategies currently operating under the efforts of problem-oriented policing. Table 3 provides a brief definition for each of the 24 categories identified in Table 2.

Table 2
Response to Identified Problems by Number and Percentage

Response	Number of Projects with Response	Percentage of Projects with Response
1. Crime Prevention Through Environmental Design	30	56.6%
2. Community Mobilization	27	50.9%
3. Targeted Enforcement Efforts	22	41.5%
4. Enforcement of Minor Violations	19	35.8%
5. Code and Licensee Enforcement	18	34.0%
6. Conveying of Information	17	32.1%
7. Use of Other City/County/State Entities	16	30.2%
8. Establishment of a Database for Identifying and Tracking of Individuals Who Are the Cause of Repeat Problems	12	22.6%
9. Enactment or Amendments of Laws/Ordinances	10	18.9%
10. Neighborhood Cleanups	10	18.9%
11. Prosecution Agreements	10	18.9%
12. Use of Private Service Providers	9	17.0%
13. Undercover Operations	9	17.0%
14. Use of Civil Legal Action	8	15.1%
15. Use of Social Service Agencies	8	15.1%
16. Establishment of Information Exchange with Schools	6	11.3%
17. Use of Media	6	11.3%
18. Use of Probation and Parole Conditions	6	11.3%
19. Joint Law Enforcement Actions	6	11.3%
22. Tenant Screening	5	9.4%
20. Establishment of Case-Handling Protocol for Sources of Repeat Problems	4	7.5%
21. Establishment of Community Centers	4	7.5%
23. Techniques to Reduce Anonymity of Law Violators	3	5.7%
24. Limiting Police Response	1	1.9%

The most common of these responses were efforts relating to crime prevention through environmental design (CPTED), community mobilization, and targeted enforcement. The categories represent a generalized classification of responses. Within each of these general categories is a diversity of specific applications. This is not unexpected. If the problem-oriented framework is properly being used, there should be some uniqueness to each response applied. The issues of intra-category diversity and exclusiveness can be better illustrated by a brief discussion of each of the top three responses.

As Table 2 indicates, CPTED was the most common response among the initiatives, with implementation in approximately 57 percent (n = 30) of the projects. However, there was no single response approach for CPTED. Each CPTED response represents an environmental modification that seeks to prevent crime. In one of the initiatives a CPTED method of removing parking meters and establishing no-parking zones in their place was used. This was done to eliminate locations for street drug dealers to hide when the police were in the area. In another initiative officers installed the hardware for video surveillance cameras at the entrance of a large multiunit housing complex, with accompanying signs alerting people to the presence of the cameras. Though the cameras were not actually working, they gave the perception of increased surveillance to the would-be law violator and, accordingly, were reported to have a suppressive effect on criminal activity. In each of these initiatives different methods were employed due to the uniqueness of the problem context, but each represented a modification to the environment in order to prevent crime and/or disorder. As a result, both of these responses, along with numerous others that were in a similar vein, were classified as a CPTED response.

Like CPTED responses, those interventions classified as community mobilization also varied in actual technique. Community mobilization is used here to mean community action that is more than simply being the "eyes and ears" of the police. Traditionally, a large portion of police work is related to responding to calls for service from citizens reporting problems. Thus, attempts to motivate citizens to report crime and disorder are difficult to discern from everyday activities. However, there are a number of techniques employed in that these initiatives took a more active approach in using citizens to address a problem. For example, one initiative involved citizens recording license plates of vehicles at a problem location on a form provided by the police. This form was then mailed to the police in order to conduct further investigation. In another initiative, various businesses and citizens donated materials, money, and time to build a center for day laborers. Each of these activities was classified as community mobilization since citizens were actively engaged in the problem response.

Table 3
Definition of Techniques

Crime Prevention Through Environmental Design – actions taken to alter a specific environment for the purpose of crime prevention and/or reduction.

Code and Licensee Enforcement – the enforcement of various local and state codes primarily related to residential dwellings or business establishments. This includes health codes, rental codes, fire codes, building codes, and alcohol license codes.

Community Mobilization – any response that actively involves residents. This requires more than actively calling the police about problems.

Conveying of Information – all activities that are related to the education of various stakeholders who are affected by the problem.

Enactment or Amendment of Laws/Ordinances – related to the creation of a new law/ordinance, or an amendment to a previously existing one that affects the problem.

Enforcement of Minor Violations – a stepped-up response to minor violations of the vehicle code, city ordinances, or other non-criminal or minor criminal violations.

Establishment of a Database for Identifying and Tracking Individuals Who Are the Cause of Repeat Problems – all actions related to the identifying and monitoring of problem-causing individuals.

Establishment of Case-Handling Protocol for Repeat Problem Sources – a response set in place to provide a scheme for handling various types of recurring events, such as a follow-up protocol for repeat domestic violence cases.

Establishment of Community Police Centers – actions that lead to the creation of community police stations. Also included are joint centers that house a community police station with members of other government services.

Establishment of Information Exchange with Schools – all cases where a regular system of notification and information exchange related to students occur between the police and school officials.

Joint Law Enforcement Actions – all responses composed of a multi-law enforcement agency response.

Limiting Police Response – actions where the police establish a criteria for limiting the response to specific calls for service.

Neighborhood Cleanups – activities carried out jointly with citizens and/ or other government entities to clean up signs of community blight.

Prosecution Agreements – arrangements between the police and local/state/federal prosecution personnel on how to handle specific cases.

Targeted Enforcement Efforts – all actions related to the increased presence and/or enforcement of criminal law by uniformed officers in specific areas. This could be an increase in various types of patrol, or suppression efforts.

Table 3, *continued*

Techniques to Reduce Anonymity of Law Violators – tactics that lead to the would-be offender recognizing that the police know of his or her presence and possible actions. This could include the use of video surveillance or other techniques, such as sending letters to vehicle owners for their car being present at a problem location.

Tenant Screening – the establishment of methods for screening out potential problem tenants at rental locations.

Undercover Operations – all enforcement activities that use plain-clothes personnel and sting operations for the purpose of criminal law enforcement.

Use of Civil Legal Action – the use of civil legal remedies to address problem locations and individuals, such as abatements and injunctions.

Use of Media – responses where the media is used to highlight progress of an effort in order to shed a positive light on a specific area, or the use of the media to focus community attention on certain problem individuals or locations.

Use of Other City/County/State Entities – all cases where other non-law enforcement state and local government agencies work in cooperation with the police to address the identified problem.

Use of Private Service Providers – responses that use various private organizations, primarily nonprofit, to assist in providing service, such as mentoring or counseling programs.

Use of Probation and Parole Conditions – joint activities where the police and probation/parole officers monitor those who have probation/parole conditions. This includes the joint enforcement of these conditions.

Use of Social Service Agencies – responses that use government social service providers to aid in addressing the problem, such as child and welfare services in the case of juvenile delinquency.

The category of targeted enforcement also included a variety of specific efforts such as increased suppression activities by officers, increased patrols (bike, foot, etc.), and traditional uniformed enforcement action against street-level drug sales. What made each of these approaches similar was that they were increased efforts by uniformed personnel in a specific area identified by the analysis of the problem. There were other responses that were similar to this category but were identified as unique in the present analysis. For example, undercover operations do include targeted enforcement efforts. However, the undercover approach often includes different personnel than uniformed patrol officers, and a different application of time and resources. The enforcement of minor violations also was singled out as a unique category, because it emphasizes not only a directed enforcement activity but also a more focused effort on those problems often associated with quality-of-life issues.

Conclusion

The primary goal of this chapter was to explore whether the nature of problems identified and the associated responses in these recognized initiatives were consistent with the broad orientation of problem-oriented policing. The findings presented suggest that this is the case. A review of the primary and related problems addressed by the various police agencies illustrates the practice of analyzing the complexity of problems that confronted communities. Further, Table 1 reveals that the award candidates were not solely focusing on traditional crime problems, and problems included truancy, cruising, and child custody disputes. In relation to the responses, some form of traditional law enforcement response (targeted enforcement, undercover operations, minor violations enforcement) was present in 64 percent (n = 34) of the initiatives. However, no initiative relied solely on criminal justice responses. The initiatives examined here represent this concept of a diverse response approach. Thus, the analysis finds that these initiatives represent a situational model of problem-oriented policing as opposed to an enforcement model.

At a more practical level, the innovation initiatives examined here hold the promise for developing a technical knowledge base of best practices, which researchers have lamented is sorely missing in the field of policing (Goldstein, 1990; Mastrofski, 1998; Sherman, 1995). This desired technical knowledge is akin to that which exists in the field of public health, whereby a problem is diagnosed and given an effective response. What is needed at this point to further develop this body of knowledge is greater collaboration between law enforcement personnel and researchers in order to gain more specific insight into when these innovating responses succeed or fail. Attention will also have to be directed at how the knowledge of these innovations can be diffused from an initial agency to the broader law enforcement community, which would include a need to understand some of the barriers and facilitators of such diffusion.

Notes

1. For additional examination of the Goldstein Award submissions, including those not recognized for awards, see Scott, 2000.

2. The Problem-Solving Partnerships (PSP) program was funded by the COPS office in 1997. The applicants were required to focus on a specific crime or disorder problem. Moreover, the law enforcement agency was generally required to partner with an outside entity, be it a nonprofit, community organization, or other local government entity. The PERF report analyzed 447 of these PSP projects.

References

Braga, A.A., D. Weisburd, E.J. Waring, L.G. Mazerolle, W. Spelman, and F. Gajewski. (1999). "Problem-Oriented Policing in Violent Crime Places: A Randomized Controlled Experiment." *Criminology* 37:541-580.

Eck, J.E. (1993). "Alternative Futures for Policing." In D. Weisburd and C. Uchida (eds.), *Police Innovation and Control of the Police: Problems of Law, Order, and Community*. New York: Springer-Verlag.

Green, L. (1996). *Policing Places with Drug Problems*. Thousand Oaks, CA: Sage.

Goldstein, H. (1979). "Improving Policing: A Problem-Oriented Approach." *Crime & Delinquency,* 25:236-258.

———— (1990). *Problem-Oriented Policing*. New York: McGraw-Hill.

Hope, T. (1994). "Problem-Oriented Policing and Drug Market Locations: Three Case Studies." In R.V. Clarke (ed.), *Crime Prevention Studies*, Vol. 2. Monsey, NY: Criminal Justice Press.

Mastrofski, S.D. (1998). "Community Policing and Police Organizational Structure." In J. Brodeur (ed.), *How to Recognize Good Policing: Problems and Issues*. Thousand Oaks, CA: Sage.

Matthews, R. (1990). "Developing More Effective Strategies to Curb Prostitution." *Security Journal* 1:182-187.

Mazerolle, L.G., J. Ready, W. Terrill, and E. Waring (2000). "Problem-Oriented Policing in Public Housing: The Jersey City Evaluations." *Justice Quarterly* 17:129-158.

National Institute of Justice (2000). *Excellence in Problem-Oriented Policing: The 2000 Herman Goldstein Award Winners*. Washington DC: National Institute of Justice.

Police Executive Research Forum (1999). Request for proposals for 1999 Herman Goldstein Award.

———— (2000). *National Evaluation of the Problem-Solving Partnership (PSP) Project*. Washington, DC: Police Executive Research Forum.

Sherman, L.W. (1995). "The Police." In J.Q. Wilson and J. Petersilia (eds.), *Crime*. San Francisco: Institute for Contemporary Studies.

Spelman, W., and J.E. Eck (1987). "Problem-Oriented Policing." *Research in Brief*. Washington, DC: National Institute of Justice.

Chapter 3

Police Problem Solving and Its Applicability to Domestic Security

Carl W. Hawkins Jr. & José M. Docobo

Introduction

On September 11, 2001, armed terrorists hijacked four airplanes and crashed them into the World Trade Center in New York City, the Pentagon in Washington, DC, and an open field in Pennsylvania. These actions not only killed thousands of innocent Americans but also angered and then rallied the people of the United States to take decisive action. How the United States would respond to this crisis and prepare to prevent future actions like these would prove very important for public safety in the United States.

In January 2002, Tom Ridge, secretary of the newly established Department of Homeland Security, stated, "Homeland security begins in your hometown." But how does local law enforcement respond to these new and demanding responsibilities and security needs? How does local law enforcement balance freedom with the steps necessary to protect its citizens? And at what cost to a free society? These questions are at the heart of debate about domestic security in the United States.

Most law enforcement agencies are better prepared today to respond to an act of terrorism than they have been in the past. They have developed detailed plans and formed partnerships with other local, state, and federal law enforcement agencies. The more important issue is not how best to respond after something terrible occurs but how to prevent such occurrences. The same approach to reducing the threat of crime, enhancing the security of our citizens, reducing fear in our communities, and improving the quality of life is also effective in terrorism prevention and deterrence. Furthermore, it is the means by which local law enforcement should conduct their daily business. The purpose of this chapter is to provide insight into how one county prepared itself to respond to terrorism and is therefore now better prepared to prevent such an incident through using problem-solving principles.

Background

Located on the Gulf Coast of Florida, Hillsborough County is a large metropolitan area with approximately 1.058 million residents and more than 1,000 square miles of land mass. The county has many features that attract visitors from all over the world. Nearly 23,000 new residents arrive to this community each year.

The county has only three incorporated cities (Tampa, Temple Terrace, and Plant City). Nearly two-thirds of the population and seven-eighths of the land mass occupy the unincorporated portion of the county. Suburban subdivisions with upscale neighborhoods in contrast to large tracts of agricultural land represent much of the real estate of the county. Hillsborough County also is home to one of the largest seaports in the southeastern United States. Cruise ships and cargo carriers make the Port of Tampa a popular destination and an attractive venue for commerce and tourism. Tampa is home to MacDill Air Force Base, which houses the strategic command center for all military operations in the Middle East, including Iraq and Afghanistan. More than 35,000 students attend the University of South Florida. Nationalities from all over the world study, teach, work, and live there. The New York Yankees make Tampa the training site for their spring baseball operations. The Tampa Bay Lightning and the Tampa Bay Buccaneers play professional hockey and football, respectively, in this community. The Outback College Football Bowl game is played on New Year's Day at Raymond James Stadium in Tampa. The Florida State Fair, the Gasparilla Pirate Fest and parade, the Plant City Strawberry Festival, and Busch Gardens round out many of the attractions that draw people to this area. These attractions also make this community a target for terrorist acts that public safety officials must contend with each day.

Problem-Solving Approach

In 1989 the Hillsborough County Sheriff's Office contracted with the Police Executive Research Forum to teach problem solving to the command staff (majors, colonels, and the sheriff). The problem-solving training program emphasized the SARA model and the crime triangle.

From 1990 to the present day, supervisors, deputies, and new recruits are taught the SARA model and the crime triangle as part of recruit, in-service, and specialized training at the agency. A standard operating procedure and a problem-analysis report have been implemented to document the problem-solving projects. A computerized program also has been developed to record all problem-solving projects and as a means to review these projects department-wide. Deputies now have a structured method for problem solving and can apply these strategies as part of their daily activities.

In addition, each area in the county has a community council working with a deputy sheriff on collaborative problem solving in their neighborhood. The close relationship between the patrol deputy and the community has formed the partnership necessary to improve the quality of life in many of these communities.

In the days immediately following September 11, 2001, the Hillsborough County Sheriff's Office redirected 13 law enforcement deputies and detectives into specific assignments related to domestic security activities. These assignments included additional staffing for K-9, aviation, marine, and intelligence units. These roles were established primarily to investigate any terrorist incident and to provide additional on-site security for the business, government, and community assets in Hillsborough County. Security assessments of the many locations within Hillsborough County were conducted within the first 90 days after September 11, 2001. These assessments sought to determine the vulnerability and security of each location so that they could be better protected from any outside threat.

Implementation of Problem Solving

During 2002, President George W. Bush gave public speeches and directed resources to the response and prevention of terrorism in the United States. President Bush outlined several actions that he believed local law enforcement should take. These included:

- Strengthening ties with Neighborhood Watch so that the local community can be the "eyes and ears" and call attention to suspicious activity.

- Recruiting citizen volunteers to help local law enforcement with the increased service demands since September 11, 2001.

- Creating a local tip line to report terrorist activities.

- Increasing technology efforts directed toward interoperability, intelligence-gathering activities, and information sharing among federal, state, and local officials.

The Immediate Response. Due to its status as Florida's second largest seaport and its close proximity to MacDill Air Force Base and downtown Tampa, the Port of Tampa was immediately identified as one of the area's most critical infrastructures for immediate protection. It was also one of the most poorly protected facilities. In the months following September 11, 2001, the Hillsborough County Sheriff's Office assigned three deputies trained in Crime Prevention Through Environmental Design and certified as crime prevention practitioners to work along with the U.S. Coast Guard in conducting approximately 29 security assessments of facilities at the Port of Tampa, most of which either store or produce large quantities of hazardous materials.

Because new Florida homeland security regulations mandated that Florida seaports provide facility security by state-certified law enforcement personnel, the port contracted with the sheriff's office for law enforcement services. Sixteen uniformed deputies began around-the-clock protection at the Port of Tampa. The deputies also received a specialized training course in terrorist response/recognition and hazardous incident response. The deputies also were issued Level B personal protective equipment, including self-contained breathing apparatus (SCBA) equipment.

Also, immediately following the events of September 11, 2001, the Florida National Guard was mobilized in order to supplement new homeland security efforts at the state's airports. It became apparent, however, that the Guard's resources were temporary and the airport would have to replace the National Guard troops with state-certified law enforcement personnel. Although Tampa International Airport has its own law enforcement agency, it was ill-equipped to hire and train sufficient numbers of new officers prior to the Guard's withdrawal. In order to meet the Transportation Safety Administration's (TSA) security mandates, Tampa International Airport turned to the Hillsborough County Sheriff's Office and the Tampa Police Department to contract for police services until such time as the airport police could hire and train the requisite number of new officers.

On May 1, 2002, eight deputies were assigned to the airport detail on a full-time basis. Ten additional deputies were assigned on a part-time basis in order to allow for vacancy control. A lieutenant and two corporals were assigned on a part-time basis to supervise personnel and monitor the contract. An equal number of personnel from the Tampa Police Department were contracted by the airport police.

Before personnel assigned to the airport were able to begin, they were required to receive training by the FBI and U.S. Customs in federal regulations and to obtain security clearances for unlimited access throughout the airport. Personnel assigned to the airport were responsible for maintaining security at the four air sides within the airport. Personnel were positioned at the screening points of each air side and were responsible for assisting screeners and other TSA personnel with security breaches and any other criminal activity that occurred at the screening post. Additionally, deputies were responsible for compliance with federal rules governing airport security and travel.

On December 1, 2002, the Hillsborough County Sheriff's Office assumed the posts previously contracted to the Tampa Police Department and continued supplying personnel until June of 2003, at which time the airport police assumed full responsibility for airport security.

Security Assessments. In addition to the certified crime prevention practitioners assigned to conduct security assessments at the Port of Tampa, personnel also were dedicated to work with each of the four patrol districts to conduct security assessments and make recommendations to critical infrastructure facilities such as water supply facilities, power plants, and telecommunication providers, as well as religious facilities, shopping centers, and other public gathering locations. With information provided by the sheriff's office district offices, a threat level manual was developed to correspond to the homeland security advisory system. This manual includes security contingencies and response guidelines for emergency response, critical infrastructure, and transportation facilities, as well as public and private schools.

In addition, the Regional Domestic Security Task Force (RDSTF) was established by executive order of the governor following September 11, 2001, to provide a systematic method within the state for allocating appropriate resources and ensuring the timely and effective dissemination of intelligence information and the investigation of possible threats to homeland security.

The RDSTF was designed around the seven existing regions for the Florida Department of Law Enforcement (FDLE) and was co-chaired by the FDLE regional director and a sheriff from each region. Hillsborough County Sheriff Cal Henderson was appointed the co-chairman of Region Four of the RDSTF. The task force members meet on a regular basis in the form of general meetings and subcommittee meetings to discuss and coordinate homeland security issues.

Additional Personnel. During September 2002, the Hillsborough County Sheriff's Office received an award from the Office of Community-Oriented Policing Services of the U.S. Department of Justice to partially fund 10 law enforcement positions through the Universal Hiring Program. Five of the positions were allocated to the marine, K-9, and intelligence units, with the five remaining positions assigned to better direct homeland security prevention efforts to the community. These services focus primarily on four programs: Neighborhood Watch, Business Watch, Worship Watch, and Volunteer Services.

Neighborhood Watch as a crime prevention tool has been in place in the United States for many years. With the understanding that the detection of criminal activity is not a job that law enforcement can do alone, Neighborhood Watch has provided extra eyes and ears in the community to report suspicious activity or crimes to law enforcement. Recognizing that the detection of suspicious behavior is an integral part of homeland security, using this already-established program has been a key part of the sheriff's office's overall homeland security effort. Staffing in this program has increased from one part-time deputy to four full-time deputies. One deputy is assigned to each of the four geographical patrol districts and is responsible for working with the community resource deputies within their assigned district to:

1. Act as a liaison with each current Neighborhood Watch group. This includes developing more efficient methods of communication between the sheriff's office and these groups in order to provide a better exchange of up-to-date crime prevention and homeland security information.

2. Recruit new Neighborhood Watch groups. Experience has shown that in areas where Neighborhood Watch groups are active, crime is generally lower and support for law enforcement is higher.

3. Review all crime-related calls for service records in their assigned area daily. Deputies will attempt to identify problem areas that can be addressed with prevention efforts. This includes working with crime analysts and district enforcement personnel seeking unified approaches in reducing crime by prevention and problem solving.

4. Meet with crime victims and other citizens to offer services to reduce their likelihood for becoming a victim in the future. The main activity supporting this task is conducting crime prevention programs and security surveys in residential areas.

5. Act as a conduit for homeland security initiatives to encourage citizens to be observant and watchful by reporting things that seem unusual or out-of-place.

Managers and business owners make risk-management decisions for their businesses every day. These risks encourage them to seek new opportunities to gain a profit. Allowing crime an opportunity to exist is not one of these risks, because no chance for profit exists when crime is present. Crime results in monetary loss, inventory loss, and a loss to the reputation of the business. Most importantly, crime can have an impact on the personal safety of employees and customers. This makes crime prevention good for business from both human and financial standpoints.

The Hillsborough County Sheriff's Office Business Watch program is modeled after the Neighborhood Watch program and establishes a formal communication network between law enforcement and businesses countywide. Business members are alerted to the potential of crime and are encouraged to look out for the community.

The sheriff's office provides members with training to educate owners, managers, and employees to be able to recognize and report any suspicious activities or crimes, to prevent shoplifting and robbery, to be a good witness, and many other topics.

Staffing of the Business Watch program consists of four full-time deputies. One deputy is assigned to each geographic enforcement district and handles all homeland security, business/commercial crime prevention, and Business Watch duties in that area. The key focus of each deputy is the delivery of proactive crime prevention and homeland security services to the business community.

Worship Watch was originally designed to bring crime prevention awareness and law enforcement services to all religious communities within Hillsborough County. This effort provides programs on personal safety, home security, drug awareness, auto theft, and many other subjects of interest to the public. Since September 11, 2001, this program has expanded from one part-time deputy to two full-time deputies. In addition, special emphasis has been placed on religious institutions that may be at greater risk because of their religious beliefs as a result of current world events.

It has long been recognized that many of the basic functions within a law enforcement agency can be accomplished by people other than sworn deputies or civilian employees. In many jurisdictions around the United States, citizens who have the time to volunteer in the community have offered their services to law enforcement agencies, freeing up personnel to spend more time in a crime-reduction role.

The Hillsborough County Sheriff's Office volunteer program is staffed with one full-time deputy who manages the current non-sworn volunteer force and acts as a recruiter for new personnel. It seeks to increase the level of civilian volunteers to supplement the office's efforts by reducing the level of workload for on-duty personnel. The coordinator is responsible for:

1. Recruiting, screening, and selecting volunteers. Determines the quality of the volunteers who join the program and serving as the person who screens for competency, responsibility, and stability. The coordinator serves as the community ambassador for the program.

2. Determining the staffing needs from the various districts and divisions throughout the sheriff's office that can benefit from the use of volunteers. The coordinator ensures the appropriate level of staffing using volunteer staff and replaces volunteers lost through attrition.

In September 2003, the Hillsborough County Sheriff's Office received a second award from the Office of Community-Oriented Policing Services of the U.S. Department of Justice to partially fund 10 law enforcement positions through the Universal Hiring Program. These positions were specifically requested to supplement operational, training, equipment, and intelligence requirements imposed by the office's efforts in homeland security. These positions were assigned in the following areas:

1. Four deputies were assigned to the marine unit, providing 24/7 marine surveillance to the Port of Tampa, with increased staffing during heightened threat periods.

2. Two detectives to serve as domestic security specialists assigned to the Regional Domestic Security Task Force. These detectives would be responsible for expanding local domestic security investigations and interagency intelligence sharing.

3. One deputy to serve as a K-9 handler specifically trained in explosives detection, to provide expanded security at the Port of Tampa and other key infrastructure locations.

4. One deputy to serve as a dedicated port security liaison. This deputy is responsible for scheduling and maintaining an optimal landside agency presence at the Port of Tampa to meet established and fluctuating public/private facility and gangway security requirements mandated by the United States Coast Guard and the Bureau of Immigration and Customs Enforcement.

5. One deputy to serve as an incident command systems/weapons of mass destruction technical equipment coordinator, responsible for the coordination, placement, and maintenance of the large amounts of specialized and highly technical domestic security equipment that the Hillsborough County Sheriff's Office has procured and must use in coordination with other public safety agencies.

6. One deputy assigned as a homeland security operations officer, responsible for promoting and ensuring common training and equipment practices, documenting agency response plans to varying domestic security threat levels, and assisting in the development of practices to ensure continuity of public safety and governmental operations.

Tipline for Terrorist Activities. The Crime Stoppers of West Central Florida Tip Line at the Hillsborough County Sheriff's Office was established as a way for residents and others in Hillsborough County to report information about who may be responsible for a crime that occurs. The tip line has been expanded to allow the public to report suspected terrorist activities. Crime Stoppers also developed a brochure and poster on what the public may look for that may be suspicious regarding possible terrorist activities. Two public buses act as roving billboards, covering different routes daily throughout Hillsborough County, with similar information on reporting possible terrorist activities. Since September 11, 2001, Crime Stoppers has referred dozens of anonymous tips concerning possible terrorist activity to law enforcement.

Information Sharing System. During the fall of 2003, the Hillsborough County Sheriff's Office initiated an information-sharing system plan for the Tampa Bay area. Meetings have been held with the six largest law enforcement agencies serving populations of greater than 100,000 people. These agencies include the Hillsborough County Sheriff's Office, the Tampa Police Department, the Pinellas County Sheriff's Office, the St. Petersburg Police Department, the Clearwater Police Department, and the Florida Department of Law Enforcement. The meetings have established a policy and procedure for information sharing, a plan to handle security issues in the information exchange, and a memorandum of understanding for the system to operate.

During 2004, the information sharing system will expand to include the smaller agencies within the two-county area. In 2005, further expansion will add additional agencies along the west coast of Florida. Based on an artificial intelligence data retrieval system developed at the University of Arizona, the system will allow law enforcement personnel to look across geographical lines to obtain information about victims, offenders, and location—the kind of information used in problem solving with the crime triangle. It will also allow agencies to solve crime and prevent future terrorist acts through the use of integrated information provided by each agency.

Community Policing Field Training Officer Program. An evaluation of the new Police Training Officer Program for Community Policing recently released by the Office of Community-Oriented Policing Services of the U.S. Department of Justice is being evaluated for implementation with the next law enforcement academy graduation in June 2004. The new training program is built around the SARA problem-solving model and will use a scenario-based instruction and demonstration methodology. Incorporating the new training system at the entry level will enable the sheriff's office to better indoctrinate all new deputies into the philosophy and tactics of community policing and problem solving from the earliest days of their work with the community.

The Future

Responding to the horrific events of September 11, 2001, enabled the Hillsborough County Sheriff's Office to better safeguard the Tampa Bay area while building on the current system of community policing and problem solving. Reducing a community's vulnerability requires assessing a jurisdiction's ability to identify possible targets and to work with community stakeholders to improve security. As time passes without future attacks, local law enforcement will find it more difficult to justify the need for specialized units or functions for what many will perceive as a passing or nonexistent threat. Agencies will therefore have to turn from preparing for a post-incident response to a new role of prevention and deterrence.

Terrorism, like crime, threatens the social order and quality of life for all citizens. Law enforcement therefore should continue to look to community policing and the tactics of problem solving, community empowerment, and relationship building to establish a structure that will provide local law enforcement with a permanent role in homeland security. This is what the Hillsborough County Sheriff's Office is doing as it prepares to respond to and deter future terrorist acts in the community. Community policing and problem solving will continue to be important components of a philosophy that should guide the direction of public safety in the United States.

Section II

Police Patrol Officer-Based Problem Solving

Chapter 4

Problem Solving Disorderly Youth*

Michael Scott

Introduction

Disorderly youth in public places constitutes one of the most common problems police agencies must handle. Dealing with youth disorder requires a significant amount of police time, particularly in suburban and rural communities. Disorderly youth are a common source of complaints from urban residents and merchants, as well as from shoppers and merchants in malls and business districts (Skogan, 1987; Beck & Willis, 1995).

Dealing with youth disorder appropriately requires considerable police skill and sensitivity. Officers must balance youths' rights against complainants' rights, distinguish legitimate from illegitimate complaints, at times be firm and at times be flexible with young people, and remain sensitive to how the public will perceive police actions.

Background

Disorderly youth in public places is only one of many disorder- and youth-related problems police must handle. This chapter addresses the relatively minor, but often highly annoying, misconduct associated with youth congregating in public. That young people will congregate in public is both inevitable and socially necessary. Congregating is part of the rite of passage

*This chapter is adapted from a POP Guide that can be accessed at www.cops.usdoj.gov/mime/ open/pdf?item=275 and was supported by cooperative agreement #2002-CK-WX-0003 by the Office of Community Oriented Policing Services, U.S. Department of Justice. The opinions contained herein are those of the author(s) and do not necessarily represent the official position of the U.S. Department of Justice.

from childhood to adulthood, allowing youth to socialize and bond with their peers, out of their parents' view. Young people's self-identity and self-worth are profoundly shaped by how they believe their peers perceive them, and gathering in public provides opportunities to see and be seen by others. Group settings provide a relatively safe context for teenagers to flirt and pair up with one another, supported and protected by their friends. Because youth congregation in public is so ordinary and normal, it must first be determined whether youths' conduct is actually disorderly and worthy of police attention. Whether the conduct is deemed disorderly depends on many factors, including the youths' specific objectionable behavior, ages, the complainants' tolerance levels, the community norms, and the specific times and places where the problem occurs.

Communities often are divided over what constitutes acceptable conduct. This is especially true in areas undergoing substantial demographic change—for example, an influx of youth where older residents have traditionally predominated, or an influx of a new ethnic or racial group. Some misconduct, even if accepted by the community, might not be tolerable from a legal standpoint. Conversely, some youth conduct may bother some community members but may be perfectly legal, perhaps even constitutionally protected. Youths' right to congregate in public must be balanced against others' right to be free from annoyance, harassment, and intimidation. Furthermore, the legal grounds for disrupting youth gatherings in public are typically vague. It is easy to become frustrated by demands to control disorderly youth where no clear legal authority to do so exists.

Young people often do not fully appreciate how their conduct affects others. What they believe to be normal and legitimate behavior can sometimes make others apprehensive or afraid. Sometimes the mere presence of large groups of youths, or their physical appearance (dress, hairstyles, body piercings, tattoos), is intimidating regardless of their conduct. People often perceive youths congregating in public to be gangs and therefore dangerous. The elderly are particularly intimidated by such large groups. In addition, group size may influence individual behavior—teenagers often behave with their peers in ways they would not if they were alone or in pairs.

Among the specific behaviors (some legal and some not) commonly associated with youth disorderly conduct are playing loud music, cursing, blocking sidewalks and streets, playing games (football, soccer, stickball, etc.) in the street or near residences, drinking alcohol, smoking and using illegal drugs, making offensive remarks to passersby, fighting, littering, drawing graffiti, vandalizing property, and harassing security staff. Such problem behavior most commonly occurs at shopping malls, in plazas within business districts, at video arcades, in public parks, on school grounds, in apartment-complex common areas, at public libraries, and at convenience stores and fast-food restaurants.

Disorderly youth are of particular concern to merchants because their presence intimidates shoppers. Shoppers also frequently cite menacing youth as among their primary safety concerns (Beck & Willis, 1995). However, young people themselves are a source of current and future revenue and, if treated poorly by merchants, will likely remember that treatment years later when choosing where to spend their money. Merchants are more likely to tolerate some disorderly behavior if the young people are also regular customers.

Youth surveys have identified some common complaints teenagers have about their opportunities to socialize in public and about how authorities treat them (National Crime Prevention, 1999; Lancashire Constabulary, 1999; Parker, 1993). Their complaints include the following: lack of adequate facilities and activities for them; harassment and excessive supervision by police and other authorities; lack of inexpensive food and entertainment; lack of adequate public transportation; inability to feel safe in public; and unfair stereotyping of them by merchants and others.

Young people typically say they want a place where they can hang out without excessive supervision, where they have some source of food and entertainment, where they have protection from the weather, and where they are safe from attack by rival groups.

Understanding the Problem

The information provided above is only a generalized description of disorderly youth in public places. These basic facts must be combined with a more specific understanding of a local problem. Analyzing the local problem carefully will help to design a more effective response strategy. To help define the problem, the police should speak with as many people affected by it as possible.

Many incidents related to disorderly youth are not recorded in detail either by police or by private security. Most incidents are considered too minor to justify detailed reports. Unfortunately, it is from those details that the most effective responses will emerge. Consequently, it should first be determined to what extent incidents are being recorded, and if they are not, a reporting system should be created that provides enough detail, at least temporarily, to provide a better understanding of the problem.

The following are some critical questions that should be asked in order to analyze a particular problem involving disorderly youth. Answers to these and other questions will help identify the most appropriate set of responses later on. The questions to ask complainants include:

- Who is complaining about the youth? What are the specific complaints?

- What are the complainants' interests (commercial, peace and quiet, freedom from intimidation)?

- Do complaints seem legitimate or exaggerated? (Some complainants exaggerate their reports of the problem in order to get a quicker or harsher police response than is justified.)

- Is there objective evidence to confirm the complaints (e.g., customers staying away from businesses, tenants moving out of apartments, reports of crimes committed by the youth)?

- Are complaints filed with police, private security, or other officials? Are complainants reluctant to file official complaints for fear of retaliation?

- Are there different cultural perspectives on the problem? (Different cultures have different expectations regarding adult supervision of youth.)

- How do complainants believe the problem could be better handled?

- What, if anything, have complainants done on their own to try to address the problem?

Questions also could be directed at youths, including:

- What are the characteristics of the young people causing the problems? How old are they? (There are significant differences between the interests and motivations of 13- to 14-year-olds and those of 20- to 21-year-olds, even though all are generally considered youth.) What race or ethnicity are the youth? Are they students? What gender are they? (Girls typically have greater parental restrictions placed on them, and they sometimes prefer to hang out indoors.) (National Crime Prevention, 1999).

- Where do the youth live? Near the place they congregate, or far away from it? How do they get there?

- Do some of the young people have serious personal problems (e.g., are they runaways, substance abusers, victims of child abuse, prostitutes, homeless)?

- How do youth perceive the problem?

- Are youth more or less manageable when they congregate in large groups? (Smaller groups may congregate in multiple locations, making them more difficult to monitor.)

- Is there any evidence that the disorderly behavior is motivated by bias (racial or otherwise)?

Finally, there are questions that need to be asked about the location and times when problem behaviors occur, such as:

- Is the location where the youth congregate urban, suburban, or rural?

- Is the location public or private property, or a mixture of both?

- Where, specifically, do the youth gather? Near entrances to businesses or other buildings? Near stairways, escalators, or other high-traffic areas?

- Are there comfortable places to sit or lean?

- Why do the youth gather where they do? For purely social reasons, or because they want to be near a particular institution (school, business, tavern, or club)? Why do they say they gather there? Do they feel they have been forced away from other locations, or is there something particular about this location that attracts them?

- What accounts for the location's attractiveness? The type of food served? Access to restrooms, telephones, video machines? Seating (e.g., tables and chairs provided for regular patrons, benches at bus stops)? Absence of a manager or other authority?

- What specific factors contribute to disorderliness (e.g., crowding, differing characteristics of youth and complainants, differing uses of public space, absence of authorities)?

- Are youth congregating where they expect to be visible to the public (and the police), or where they do not expect to be seen?

- Does the manager of the place where youth congregate tolerate disorderly behavior more than seems reasonable? (If so, the manager may be involved in illicit conduct for which the youth offer some protection.) (Meehan, 1992).

Problem-Solving Approach

Once a problem has been identified, it is important to measure its scope. Measurement allows police departments to determine the extent to which specific efforts have succeeded, and suggests how responses might be modified if they are not producing the intended results. The following are potentially useful measures of the effectiveness of responses to disorderly youth in public places:

- reduced recorded crime and disorder incidents related to youth in public places;

- reduced calls for police service related to youth in public places (increased reports to officials or reduced anonymous complaints may initially be a positive indicator if you determine that complainants have previously been reluctant to come forward);

- reduced numbers of young people congregating at particular locations (if crowd size contributes to the disorderliness);

- reduced numbers of repeat offenders;

- improved perceptions of complainants (merchants, shoppers, residents);

- improved perceptions of elected officials, who often receive complaints about juvenile disorder;

- improved perceptions of youth regarding how fairly they are treated;

- improved perceptions of parents regarding their children's conduct and police treatment of their children;

- reduced costs for repairs due to vandalism (if vandalism is part of the problem);

- evidence of displacement of the problem to other locations (where complaints may be higher or lower); and

- evidence of reduced youth disorder-related crimes and complaints in areas not directly targeted by your initiative (otherwise known as a *diffusion of benefits*).

An analysis of a problem should provide a better understanding of the factors contributing to it. Once a problem has been analyzed and means established for measuring effectiveness, the possible responses to the problem should be considered. In most cases, an effective strategy will involve implementing several different responses, because law enforcement responses alone are seldom effective in reducing or solving a problem.

There are three general approaches to addressing problems of disorderly youth in public places: (1) a *pure control approach*, which views the youth as offenders whose conduct is to be controlled and prohibited coercively; (2) a *developmental approach*, which views the youth more neutrally and adopts methods that, in addition to controlling misconduct, seeks to improve the youths' general welfare; and (3) an *accommodation approach*, which balances the youths' needs and desires against the complainants' needs and desires (National Crime Prevention, 1999).

Whenever possible, the developmental and accommodation approaches are recommended, because they are more likely to be effective and they reduce mistrust and hostility between youth and authority figures, including police (White, 1998). The general public and the media tend to react negatively to what they perceive as heavy-handed police responses against youth. Parents commonly complain when police resort to arrest as a means of solving youth disorder problems. Some young people may even find the extra efforts of police and others to control their conduct exciting—a game of cat and mouse—making disorderly behavior even more appealing to them (White & Sutton, 1995).

Responses

The following are specific responses that police and others have applied to youth disorder in public. These responses variously incorporate pure control, developmental, and accommodation approaches. They are organized into three categories: (1) creating alternative legitimate places and activities for youth; (2) modifying public places to discourage disorderly behavior; and (3) establishing and enforcing rules of conduct for youth.

Creating Alternative Legitimate Places and Activities for Youth

1. **Creating new places for youth to congregate and providing alternative activities**. Recognizing that most young people want to hang out with their peers without excessive adult supervision, some police agencies have supported youth clubs, drop-in centers, or recreation centers to attract youth who otherwise would be creating public disorder (Bland & Read, 2000); Lancashire Constabulary, 1999; Ball, 1994). In England, the Lancashire police arranged for youth to help an architect design a public youth shelter (Lancashire Constabulary, 1999).

   Some shopping malls operate centers where youth can hang out without disturbing shoppers (Poole, 1991). Some police officers have helped to organize alternative constructive activities for young people, such as youth clubs or athletic programs, and have given youth an active role in managing these programs (New York City Police Department, 1993; Lancashire Constabulary, 1999) Cleveland Police, 1998).

2. **Providing outreach services to youth.** In addition to needing recreation, entertainment, and a place to socialize, some young people need health, legal, and social services that they do not or cannot obtain through normal channels. Some youth who create public disorder are supported by stable families, but others are not. Some are runaways, substance abusers, victims of child neglect and abuse, homeless, or prostitutes. Police can support initiatives to provide outreach services to youth (Lancashire Constabulary, 1999). These services can be an effective bridge between youth and formal authorities like the police (Phillips & Cochrane, 1988; Bland & Read, 2000; White, 1998; Poole, 1991). Outreach workers can help identify particular needs of youth groups and individuals and can broker services and assistance for them. They can also remind youth to behave appropriately in public, without threatening them with enforcement.

3. **Employing youth at businesses negatively affected by disorderly behavior.** Some merchants have succeeded in reducing the incidence of youth disorder by employing qualified youth to work in establishments near where young people congregate. The employed youth have a greater sense of responsibility for, and stake in, maintaining order (Phillips & Cochrane, 1988; White, 1998; Ball, 1994).

4. **Ensuring youth have adequate transportation to and from events**. Event planners and parents do not always provide adequate transportation for youth, leaving large numbers of young people unsupervised on the streets before and after events. Special-event and youth program managers should be encouraged to factor transportation costs into their financial calculations. Police in Newport News, Virginia, addressed a problem of disorderly youths leaving a roller skating rink late at night by ensuring adequate transportation for them at closing time (Eck & Spelman, 1987).

Modifying Public Places to Discourage Disorderly Behavior

5. **Encouraging youth to gather where they will not disturb others.** If youth are congregating near a particular institution (school, business, tavern, or club), they should be encouraged to work with the institution to move where their behavior will not disturb others. If rival groups are gathering at the same location, the groups should be persuaded to change the times when they gather or try to get one group to congregate elsewhere. Some officers have had bus stops relocated to prevent conflicts between rival youth groups. A Joliet, Illinois, police officer negotiated with a stadium owner to let youth congregate in a section of the stadium parking lot (Parker, 1993). Many police officers negotiate informal agreements with youth—for example, exchanging a degree of tolerance of rowdy behavior for keeping noise and litter under control (Meehan, 1992).

6. **Avoiding locating businesses that attract youth where others will be intimidated by them**. This response applies mainly to shopping malls where mall managers can determine the specific location of businesses. Fast-food restaurants and video arcades commonly attract large groups of youths. If they are located near mall entrances and exits or along heavily traveled pathways, shoppers are forced to walk past the youth, and the potential for intimidation rises (Poole, 1991). Without training, mall managers may not have a good understanding of how design features and business locations can affect crime and disorder levels (Poole, 1991).

7. **Reducing the comfort level, convenience, or attraction of popular youth gathering places.** Eliminating comfortable places to sit or lean discourages youth from congregating in particular places (although it might prove a similar inconvenience for others) (Poole, 1991). If the location is outdoors, consider modifying structures (bus shelters, shop doorways, playground equipment, park shelters, pedestrian tunnels, covered alleys, bridges) so that they do not offer much protection from the weather (Lancashire Constabulary, 1999).

    The type of background music also can influence where youth choose to congregate: playing classical music, for example, can discourage some young people from hanging out within earshot of a location (Chambers, 1991).

    Intensifying the lighting where youth congregate also can make the location less attractive to them (New York City Police Department, 1993). Police in Edmonton, Alberta, worked with the community and other city agencies to landscape a park that had become a hangout for older youth who intimidated other park users and vandalized park property. The new park configuration made it more visible from adjacent roads. Problems declined without the need for extra police enforcement (Cooper & Kracher, 1996). Police in Peel, Ontario, worked with school officials to redesign the school parking lot and hallways, thereby significantly reducing disorder problems caused by students and trespassers (McKay, 1997). Police in Delta, British Columbia, determined that the physical layout of the video arcades influenced youth disorder levels in and around them. They proposed local legislation that regulates video arcade design in ways that improve arcade employees' ability to monitor youth conduct.

    If youth rely on cars to get to the location, or if cars are the attraction (part of a street-cruising problem), consider altering parking regulations to limit youths' ability to gather a lot of cars in one place (New York City Police Department, 1993).

8. **Installing and monitoring closed-circuit television (CCTV) cameras.** CCTV, used extensively in the United Kingdom and generally supported by merchants, shoppers, and the general public, has shown some effectiveness in controlling youth disorder in public places (Brown, 1997). A Scottish study concluded that a CCTV camera positioned in a public town center had the effect of moving disorder incidents out of the camera's view, keeping fights among youth briefer, and with fewer combatants. Overall, the CCTV reduced the actual number of disorder incidents, although the study noted that the number of recorded incidents might well rise due to the increased CCTV monitoring (Ditton & Short, 1998) *see also* Ditton and Short, 1999). Another U.K. study concluded that CCTV was more useful for alerting police to disorder incidents than for deterring disorder in the first place (Oc & Tiesdell, 1997).

Establishing and Enforcing Rules of Conduct for Youth

9.   **Enlisting others to exercise informal social control over youth.**
     Informal social control that others can exercise over young peo-
     ple should be encouraged. Parents, school officials, employers,
     coaches, and others should be enlisted to establish and enforce
     standards of youth conduct in public. Research has established that
     people who are responsible for managing places—whether malls,
     businesses, apartment buildings, commercial districts, or parks—
     can collectively act to enforce rules and standards of orderly
     behavior that result in reduced disorder (Mazerolle, Kadleck &
     Roehl, 1998).

     Police can notify people, in person or in writing, about indi-
     viduals causing problems. Officers in Manchester, England, dis-
     tributed a leaflet to parents explaining the problems, police
     responses, parental responsibilities, and potential consequences for
     failing to control their children's behavior (including sanctions
     against their public housing) (Bland & Read, 2000; Lancashire
     Police Constabulary, 1999; Cleveland Police, 1998). Police in
     Lancashire, England, videotaped disorderly youth and showed
     the videotapes to their parents (Bland & Read, 2000; Lancashire
     Police Constabulary, 1999). Many jurisdictions have parental
     responsibility laws with sanctions against parents who fail to
     exercise reasonable control over their children's conduct; however,
     these laws are rarely enforced.

10. **Establishing clear rules of conduct and educating youth about
     them.** Patrol officers usually develop their own personal standards
     for youth conduct that they pass on to the youth by word or action.
     Unfortunately, the same youth are subject to many different patrol
     officers' standards. When the standards change depending on
     which officer is on duty, youth perceive the standards to be arbi-
     trary and therefore unfair (Meehan, 1992). Officers should work
     together to devise a reasonably consistent set of standards for
     dealing with congregating youth.

     Shopping mall managers should establish a clear set of rules
     of conduct and post them where youth congregate. Some merchants
     impose minimum-purchase requirements or restrict restroom use
     to paying customers to discourage youth from gathering outside
     their businesses. Some malls have resorted to requiring teenagers
     to have parental escorts during certain hours.

     Some Dutch police visit schools at the beginning of the school
     year to inform students about rules of conduct that will apply in
     places where students are known to hang out (Phillips & Cochrane,
     1988; *see also* Parker, 1993). Lancashire police instituted a juve-
     nile nuisance register to log police officers' warnings to young peo-
     ple and justify harsher responses if the youth ignored the warnings
     (Bland & Read, 2000; Lancashire Police Constabulary, 1999).

11. **Mediating conflicts between youth and complainants.** As noted earlier, young people often fail to appreciate their behavior's effect on others. Bringing youth and complainants together can result in a healthy exchange of perspectives. In some instances, complainants have been known to become more sympathetic to the lack of opportunities for youth and are willing to help provide them (Phillips & Cochrane, 1988; Bland & Rea, 2000; Cleveland Police, 1998; Ball, 1994). If there is racial or ethnic bias to the complaints, professional cultural awareness training for complainants and youth should be provided (New York City Police Department, 1993).

12. **Denying youths' anonymity.** In some instances, simply getting to know the names and faces of young people, thereby removing their sense of anonymity, is sufficient to discourage them from causing trouble (Poole, 1991). Without being antagonistic or accusatory, police and private security officers can make special efforts to let youth know they can readily be identified. In some instances, police and private security have resorted to photographing and identifying youth who create disturbances, either as part of an official trespass warning system, or merely to put the troublemakers on notice that their conduct is being monitored (Eck & Spelman, 1987).

13. **Deploying police paraprofessionals to patrol public places where youth congregate.** Police in the Netherlands and the United Kingdom hire and assign uniformed paraprofessionals—variously called wardens, special constables, or patrollers—to patrol public places where youth often congregate (Hofstra & Shapland, 1997; Southgate, Bucke, and Byron, 1995; Lancashire Police Constabulary, 1999; Jacobson and Saville, 1999). Evaluations of these paraprofessionals' effectiveness have shown some reductions in citizen fear and complaints about youth disorder in the areas patrolled (Hofstra & Shapland, 1997; Southgate, Bucke & Byron, 1995; Jacobson & Saville, 1999), but at least in the United Kingdom, the paraprofessionals were not well received by either the police or the general public (Southgate, Bucke & Byron, 1995). Their effectiveness appears to depend on their being reasonable and approachable rather than trying to be intimidating (Hofstra & Shapland, 1997). Some police agencies have supported citizen patrols to help monitor young people's behavior in public (Bland & Read, 2000).

    Private security officers constitute one type of paraprofessional, and while they tend to be dressed and equipped like police officers, some youth are more likely to challenge their authority and try to provoke confrontations if they resemble police (Poole, 1991). Police might provide training to private security in handling youth in public places (Phillips & Cochrane, 1988).

14. **Enforcing truancy laws.** Truancy enforcement can be effective in reducing youth disorder occurring during school hours (Bland & Read, 2000; Lancashire Police Constabulary, 1999; Poole, 1991; Books, 1995). Police can educate complainants about truancy laws so that they know when and how to notify authorities about truancy violations. However, truancy enforcement, while an increasingly popular idea, is not necessarily an appropriate response to your particular disorderly youth problem. In order for it to be effective, school officials and other juvenile authorities must cooperate with police and develop practices and programs that prevent truancy, while addressing underlying problems that might cause habitual truancy. Police agencies should establish specific policies and procedures for truancy enforcement rather than relying on occasional and highly discretionary enforcement.

15. **Enforcing curfew laws.** Curfew laws are intended to keep youth off the streets at night, so that they are more likely to be under adult supervision at home. Some jurisdictions, such as Orlando, Florida, have imposed curfews on juveniles only in the downtown entertainment districts, where problems have been concentrated. Whether curfew enforcement is effective at reducing youth disorder depends on particular local conditions (White, 1998; Bland & Read, 2000). In many jurisdictions, youth are more likely to cause trouble after school than at night (White, 1998).

    Proposals to enact or enforce juvenile curfews almost always inspire community debate. The general public and presumably young people themselves are more likely to accept curfews if alternative legitimate activities and places for youth to gather exist (White, 1998). If police are expected to enforce juvenile curfews, there must be convenient holding facilities that allow officers to return to the streets quickly; otherwise, they are not likely to take juveniles into custody. As with truancy enforcement, police agencies that opt to enforce curfew laws should establish specific policies and procedures relating to enforcement.

16. **Banning troublemakers from private property.** If youth are congregating and creating disturbances on privately owned property, such as business parking lots or apartment complexes, you might consider securing authority from the property owners for the police to enforce trespass laws.

    Trespass enforcement was one of a combination of responses that St. Petersburg, Florida, police used to reduce problems caused by students gathering in a convenience store parking lot. Stricter truancy enforcement by school officials and turning off video games in the convenience store during school hours were the other key responses (Books, 1995). Newport News, Virginia, police also used trespass enforcement to deal with disorderly youth at a shopping plaza, and encouraged judges to order convicted offenders to stay away from the plaza as a condition of a suspended sentence (Eck & Spelman, 1987).

Shopping malls are generally considered private rather than public places, giving mall owners and managers greater legal authority to deny access to the premises, but in many jurisdictions they are considered quasi-public. Police agencies should establish specific policy guidelines that cover police officers' authority and responsibilities in helping mall authorities enforce the bans in a prudent manner. Identities of banned youth should be provided to merchants and security staff.

Responses with Limited Effectiveness

17. **Increasing patrol by uniformed police officers.** Merely increasing uniformed police officers' presence around locations where youth gather is expensive, inefficient, and usually ineffective.

18. **Strictly enforcing laws against youth.** Many police officers are hesitant to rely excessively on arrest as a means of controlling troublesome youth behavior. Where juvenile justice system sanctions are lenient, as they often are for minor offenses, officers prefer not to expose youth to that leniency, hoping that they will believe the sanctions to be serious (Meehan, 1992). It may be necessary to strictly enforce some laws, at least for a while, just to convince youth that the option is available. Done properly, some enforcement can open lines of communication between the police and young people who might question law enforcement authority to act (New York City Police Department, 1993).

Conclusion

The table below summarizes the responses to disorderly youth in public places, the mechanism by which they are intended to work, the conditions under which they should work best, and some factors that should be considered before implementing a particular response. It is critical that these responses be tailored to local circumstances, and that each can be justified based on reliable analysis. In most cases, an effective strategy will involve implementing several different responses. Law enforcement responses alone are seldom effective in reducing or solving the problem.

Creating Alternative Legitimate Places and Activities for Youth

Response	How It Works	Works Best If . . .	Considerations
Creating new places for youth to congregate and providing alternative activities	Removes excuses for youth to hang out and be disorderly in public, for lack of anything else to do	. . . there are few or no alternative legitimate activities for youth in the area	Police can support creating alternative places and activities, but should be careful not to become solely responsible for running those places and activities
Providing outreach services to youth	Identifies more serious problems of some youth, such as substance abuse, child abuse, mental illness, etc.	. . . the young people causing the problems are suspected to have more serious individual problems and needs	Requires resource commitments from professionals outside the police department
Employing youth at businesses negatively affected by disorderly behavior	Promotes a greater sense of responsibility among youth for maintaining order in those places	. . . there is viable employment in the area, and young people have skills that match employers' needs	Business owners must be willing to employ youth
Ensuring youth have adequate transportation to and from events	Removes excuses for youth to be on the street before and after events	. . . √existing transportation is inadequate	May require additional expenditures from public transportation companies

Modifying Public Places to Discourage Disorderly Behavior

Response	How It Works	Works Best If . . .	Considerations
Encouraging youth to gather where they will not disturb others	Separates youth from likely complainants	. . . there are viable alternative places for youth to gather in the area	May require negotiation because police may not be able to force youth to move; may require place managers' or property owners' cooperation to allow youth to congregate
Avoiding locating businesses that attract youth where others will be intimidated by them	Separates youth from likely complainants	. . . there are alternative sites for the youth-oriented businesses	Requires the cooperation of people such as mall managers; youth-oriented businesses may object to being moved away from the main flow of consumers
Reducing the comfort level, convenience, or attraction of popular youth gathering places	Discourages youth from congregating in a particular place	. . . the changes are not unduly burdensome on legitimate users of the place	May require additional expenditures to redesign the place; may discourage legitimate uses of the place; may displace youth to a more problematic location
Installing and monitoring closed-circuit television (CCTV) cameras	Increases the ability of police or private security to detect disorder and respond quickly; increases the likelihood that offenders can be identified later; discourages youth from engaging in disorderly behavior in view of the camera	. . . police or private security has the resources to monitor CCTV	Cameras must be protected from vandalism; monitoring is labor-intensive; evaluations of CCTV show mixed effectiveness; some communities object to public CCTV on privacy grounds

Establishing and Enforcing Rules of Conduct for Youth

Response	How It Works	Works Best If . . .	Considerations
Enlisting others to exercise informal social control over youth	Provides help from others in controlling youth	. . . youth value their relationship with those seeking to exercise informal social control over them	Police must be careful not to support draconian or abusive forms of punishment
Establishing clear rules of conduct, and educating youth about them	Clarifies what conduct is and is not acceptable; removes excuses for unacceptable behavior	. . . rules are simple, fair, and clearly conveyed	Rules must not violate youths' constitutional rights; if youth perceive rules to be unfair, it may exacerbate tension and mistrust between youth and authorities, including police
Mediating conflicts between youth and complainants	Helps youth and complainants better understand one another's concerns and perspectives	. . . youth and complainants are willing to listen to one another, and conflicts are relatively minor	Requires mediation skills; may not be a valid response if offenses are serious
Denying youths' anonymity	Makes youth realize they can be held accountable for their actions	. . . the same individuals return to the problem location, and the same police or security officers handle the problem	Compulsory identification and photographing of offenders must comply with applicable laws and policies
Deploying police paraprofessionals to patrol public places where youth congregate	Increases the level of surveillance of public places; imposes supervision on youth that is not as threatening to them as police supervision might be	. . . paraprofessionals are authorized by local law to patrol in public and are properly trained to handle youth disorder	Neither the police nor the general public may support paraprofessionals
Enforcing truancy laws	Removes excuses for youth to be on the street during school hours	. . . there is a place where police can bring truants and quickly return to service, there are meaningful truancy interventions by schools, and likely complainants are educated about truancy laws and how to recognize and report truants	Requires support and resource commitments from school officials and other juvenile authorities
Enforcing curfew laws	Removes excuses for youth to be on the street at night, thereby reducing opportunities for them to offend and be victimized	. . . the general public supports curfew enforcement, and youth disorder occurs at night	Potential legal challenges to curfew laws and enforcement thereof; without public support, the police will appear heavy-handed and youth will be perceived as victims
Banning troublemakers from private property	Removes the worst offenders from places where they disturb others	. . . private security and police maintain accurate records of banned individuals' identities and the periods for which those people are banned	Potential legal challenges to banning that may depend on whether the property is deemed private or quasi-public

Responses with Limited Effectiveness

Response	How It Works	Works Best If . . .	Considerations
Increasing patrol by uniformed police officers			Labor-intensive and only temporarily effective
Strictly enforcing laws against youth			Labor-intensive as a long-term strategy; police risk losing public support by appearing heavy-handed

References

Ball, M. (1994). *Public Nuisance Offences: An Integrated Approach.* London: Home Office Police Research Group.

Beck, A., and A. Willis (1995). *Crime and Security: Managing the Risk to Safe Shopping.* Leicester, UK: Perpetuity Press.

Bland, N., and T. Read (2000). *Policing Anti-Social Behaviour.* London: Home Office Policing and Reducing Crime Unit.

Books, J. (1995). "Store No Longer a Hangout for Disorderly Teens." *Problem-Solving Quarterly* 8(3/4):7.

Brown, B. (1997). "CCTV in Three Town Centers in England." In R. Clarke (ed.), *Situational Crime Prevention: Successful Case Studies,* Second Edition. Guilderland, NY: Harrow and Heston.

Chambers, T. (1991). "Eliminating Problems Through Environmental Design." *Problem-Solving Quarterly* 5(1):9.

Cleveland (UK) Police (1998). "Raby Rebels Youth Project." Submission for the Herman Goldstein Award for Excellence in Problem-Oriented Policing.

Cooper, R., and R. Kracher (1996). "Remaking a Playground." *Problem-Solving Quarterly* 9(1/2):1-3.

Ditton, J., and E. Short (1999). "Yes, It Works, No, It Doesn't: Comparing the Effects of Open-Street CCTV in Two Adjacent Scottish Town Centres." In K. Painter and N. Tilley (eds.), *Surveillance of Public Space: CCTV, Street Lighting and Crime Prevention. Crime Prevention Studies, Vol. 10.* Monsey, NY: Criminal Justice Press.

———— (1998). "Evaluating Scotland's First Town Centre CCTV Scheme." In C. Norris, J. Moran, and G. Armstrong (eds.), *Surveillance, Closed-Circuit Television and Social Control.* Hants, UK: Ashgate.

Eck, J., and W. Spelman (1987). *Problem-Solving: Problem-Oriented Policing in Newport News.* Washington, DC: Police Executive Research Forum.

Hofstra, B., and J. Shapland (1997). "Who Is in Control?" *Policing and Society* 6(4):265-281.

Jacobson, J., and E. Saville (1999). *Neighbourhood Warden Schemes: An Overview.* Crime Reduction Research Series. London: Home Office.

Kenney, D., and T. Watson (1998). "Reducing Fear in the Schools: Managing Conflict with Student Problem-Solving." In T. Shelley and A. Grant (eds.), *Problem-Oriented Policing: Crime-Specific Problems, Critical Issues and Making POP Work.* Washington, DC: Police Executive Research Forum.

Lancashire Constabulary (1999). "The M.A.N.E.R.S. Project: The Multiagency Nuisance Eradication Scheme." Submission for the Herman Goldstein Award for Excellence in Problem-Oriented Policing.

Mazerolle, L., C. Kadleck, and J. Roehl (1998). "Controlling Drug and Disorder Problems: The Role of Place Managers." *Criminology* 36(2):371-403.

McKay, T. (1997). "Environmental Changes Bring Order to School Campus." *Problem-Solving Quarterly* 10(1):1, 8-9.

Meehan, A. (1992). " 'I Don't Prevent Crime, I Prevent Calls': Policing as a Negotiated Order." *Symbolic Interaction* 15(4):455-480.

National Crime Prevention (1999). *Hanging Out: Negotiating Young People's Use of Public Space.* Canberra, Australia: National Crime Prevention, Attorney-General's Department.

New York City Police Department (1993). *Disorderly Groups: Problem-Solving Annual for Community Police Officers and Supervisors.* New York: New York City Police Department.

O'Brien, L., and P. Joseph (1999). "Are Juvenile Curfews a Legal and Effective Way To Reduce Juvenile Crime?" In J. Sewell (ed.), *Controversial Issues in Policing.* Boston: Allyn and Bacon.

Oc, T., and S. Tiesdell (eds.) (1997). *Safer City Centres: Reviving the Public Realm.* London: Paul Chapman Publishing.

Painter, K., and N. Tilley (eds.) (1999). *Surveillance of Public Space: CCTV, Street Lighting and Crime Prevention. Crime Prevention Studies,* Vol. 10. Monsey, NY: Criminal Justice Press.

Parker, P. (1993). "Mediation with the Congregation: Property Owners Praise POP Efforts Aimed at Youth Gatherings." *Police* (March):26-27.

Phillips, S., and R. Cochrane (1988). *Crime and Nuisance in the Shopping Centre: A Case Study in Crime Prevention.* London: Home Office Crime Prevention Unit.

Poole, R. (1991). *Safer Shopping: The Identification of Opportunities for Crime and Disorder in Covered Shopping Centres.* London: Home Office Police Requirements Support Unit.

Sheard, M. (1998). "The Elite Arcade: Taming a Crime Generator." *Problem-Solving Quarterly* 11(2):1-4.

Skogan, W. (1987). *Disorder and Community Decline.* Evanston, IL: Center for Urban Affairs and Police Research, Northwestern University.

Southgate, P., T. Bucke, and C. Byron (1995). *The Parish Special Constables Scheme.* London: Home Office Research and Statistics Department.

White, R. (1998). "Curtailing Youth: A Critique of Coercive Crime Prevention." In L. Mazerolle and J. Roehl (eds.), *Civil Remedies and Crime Prevention. Crime Prevention Studies,* Vol. 9. Monsey, NY: Criminal Justice Press.

White, R., and A. Sutton (1995). "Crime Prevention, Urban Space and Social Exclusion." *Australian and New Zealand Journal of Sociology* 31(1):81-99.

Chapter 5

Problem Solving Auto Theft in Unincorporated Hillsborough County, Florida: Ten Years of Data*

Carl W. Hawkins Jr.

Introduction

Beginning in 1990, juvenile crime in Florida skyrocketed, fueling an explosion in property crimes. In unincorporated Hillsborough County, juveniles turned to auto theft as one of their main criminal activities. By the early 1990s, auto theft had risen 71 percent to its highest level in the county's history, and unincorporated Hillsborough County achieved notoriety as having the second highest auto theft rate in the state. Citizens were alarmed by the growing auto theft problem, and they expressed their concern through phone calls, letters, and at community meetings with the sheriff's office.

Both the community and the local news media urged the sheriff's office to find a solution to the growing problem of auto theft after traditional strategies implemented throughout this period failed to make a substantial impact. For example, the Hillsborough County Sheriff's Office deployed specific street-crime squads targeting areas where cars were stolen. An agency-wide auto theft task force was implemented to combat this situation. Also, auto theft detectives concentrated their efforts on auto salvage yards where motor vehicles were being chopped into parts. While these methods were somewhat successful, a smarter and more effective approach was needed.

---

*This chapter is adapted from an article that originally appeared in *Community Policing in a Rural Setting*, Second Edition, by Quint C. Thurman and Edmund F. McGarrell (eds.), copyright © 2003 by Anderson Publishing Co.

Background

Located on the west coast of Florida, unincorporated Hillsborough County is a large suburban/rural community with one of the largest cargo ports in the southeastern United States. With only three incorporated cities (Tampa, Temple Terrace, and Plant City), nearly two-thirds of the population and seven-eighths of the land mass occupy the unincorporated portion of the county. Suburban subdivisions with upscale neighborhoods contrast with large tracts of agricultural land represent much of the real estate of this county. Housing starts, tourism, cruise lines, container transport, and commodities such as strawberries, tomatoes, citrus, beef, poultry, and dairy products represent the major economic fuel behind the population growth and economic development of unincorporated Hillsborough County.

Problem-Solving Approach

In 1989 the Hillsborough County Sheriff's Office contracted with the Police Executive Research Forum to teach problem solving to the command staff (majors, colonels, and the sheriff). From 1990 to 1993, supervisors, deputies, and new recruits were taught the SARA model and the crime triangle as part of a new training course. A standard operating procedure and a problem analysis report were created to provide a way to document problem-solving projects. A problem analysis advisory committee was developed to review the various problem-solving projects. A library for past projects was established. Deputies now had a place to review similar projects for ideas that could be helpful in solving the problems they were working on. They also had a structured method for problem solving and could apply these strategies as part of their daily job.

Following this, in 1993 a community policing model that focused on the core components of community engagement and problem solving was implemented. This model gave deputies ownership of community resource areas. The deputies subsequently identified 26 neighborhoods in unincorporated Hillsborough County where calls for service and problems were concentrated.

Each area had a community council that worked with a deputy on collaborative problem solving in their neighborhoods. Surveys administered to citizens in 1994 and 1995 in the resource areas listed auto theft as one of the most important problems facing these communities. The community resource deputies began working on this problem. Recognizing that auto theft was not unique to a given neighborhood but consistent as a problem across the county, an agency-wide collaborative strategy was needed.

Drawing upon the sheriff's office's problem-solving experience, two agency-wide strategies were developed to reduce the number of auto thefts in unincorporated Hillsborough County. These were Operation "HEAT" (Help Eliminate Auto Theft) and "Training, Education, and Apprehension—A Three-Pronged Attack on Auto Theft."

Implementation of Problem Solving

In 1993, Operation HEAT was initiated. The focus of this strategy was on education and public awareness of the auto theft problem, strategies to prevent motor vehicles from being stolen, and the consequences of being arrested for this crime. In unincorporated Hillsborough County, juveniles represented the largest group stealing motor vehicles. Information was obtained on where motor vehicles were taken from and the makes and models stolen most often. The information was then printed on trifold handouts and provided to deputies to help them in teaching the training classes.

Motor vehicles were stolen from:

- driveways of single-family dwellings, or from apartment complex parking lots or parking garages (50%)

- parking lots or parking garages (36%)

- stores or shopping malls (8%)

- hotels or motels (3%)

- office buildings (2%)

- schools, universities, or nightclubs (1%)

The vehicles most commonly stolen were:

Make	Model
Chevrolet (20.6%)	Camaro (7.1%)
	Monte Carlo (3%)
	Caprice (2.4%)
	Celebrity (1.8%)
Pontiac (12%)	Grand Prix (4.1%)
	Trans Am (2.4%)
Oldsmobile (10.9%)	Cutlass (4.7%)
Ford (9.2%)	Pickup (3%)
Buick (8.7%)	Regal (4.7%)
Mazda (4.3%)	RX-7 (4.7%)
Cadillac (3.8%)	
Honda (3.8%)	Accord (2.4%)
Toyota (3.8%)	
Jeep (3.3%)	Cherokee (2.4%)
All Others (19.6%)	

Training classes were offered at community meetings (potential victims) on the problem of auto theft and ways to prevent their motor vehicles from being stolen. Additional classes were offered at the middle schools to educate the youth (potential offenders) on the consequences of this crime. Steering wheel locking mechanisms were also given away during the training class. Two professionally developed videos aimed at potential victims and juveniles were used during the instruction. Billboards, posters, displays, and bilingual trifold handouts were distributed in the target areas. A tip line was established by the sheriff's office, and rewards were given for information leading to the arrest of those responsible for stealing cars.

In 1996 a second strategy to reduce auto theft was added. "Training, Education, and Apprehension—A Three-Pronged Attack on Auto Theft" concentrated on a comprehensive specialized auto theft training program taught to deputies, detectives, other law enforcement agencies, and the state attorney's office. Additional educational programs were offered to citizens in the areas where auto thefts were concentrated. Collaboration among the sheriff's office, U.S. Customs Service, Tampa Port Authority, and the Seaboard Tampa Terminals was instituted to apprehend those responsible for stealing motor vehicles in unincorporated Hillsborough County. This strategy expanded the efforts of Operation HEAT but also went after adult criminals.

To help with this effort, the sheriff's office, other agency personnel, and the state attorney's office of Hillsborough County attended specialized training classes. Also, technical equipment (i.e., vehicle identification number verifier systems, night vision devices, digital zoom cameras, camcorders, and reference manuals for auto theft investigations) was purchased. In addition, unannounced inspections of the cargo ports and railroad yards in Tampa were implemented to reduce an avenue of distribution for stolen motor vehicles.

Results

With the implementation of Operation HEAT (1993, 1994, and 1995) and "Training, Education, and Apprehension—A Three-Pronged Attack on Auto Theft" (1996, 1997, and 1998), auto thefts decreased by 68 percent, or 1,680 reported stolen motor vehicles, between 1994 and 1998. This represented the largest decrease in stolen automobiles in the past decade. Although subsequent interviews determined that auto theft was no longer a major problem in many of the community resource areas at this time, starting in 1999, unincorporated Hillsborough County saw a slight increase in this type of crime and auto thefts began to creep upward. From 1999 to 2002, auto theft rose by eight percent, or 346 additional stolen cars.

To counter this increase, the Hillsborough County Sheriff's Office continued their problem-solving strategies but centralized all auto theft detectives into one division. Because auto theft was not geographically concentrated or bound by turf, it was determined that information could be better coordinated throughout the agency from one source rather than four divisions as before.

The Sheriff's Crime Information Strategy System (SCISS) also was implemented during this time. Patterned after COMPSTAT (computer comparison statistics) in New York City, strategy sessions were conducted on a regular basis, combining agency resources to deal with problems that may occur within a specific area. Bringing together community resource deputies, detectives, intelligence detectives, crime analysts, and specific command personnel, additional information was developed to better coordinate the efforts of all auto theft initiatives and to identify other problems and strategies to resolve.

During the first 11 months of 2003, auto theft declined by 9.1 percent, or 360 auto thefts, compared to the first 11 months of 2002. With problem-solving strategies in place, the collaborative partnerships formed, the centralization of auto theft detectives within a unified command, and the implementation of SCISS, the sheriff's office now has an agency-wide problem-solving strategy that appears to be working.

Conclusion

Auto theft is a problem in many growing communities and regions across the United States. In unincorporated Hillsborough County, auto theft was prompted by a rapid increase in juvenile crime and a large cargo port and railroad yard for domestic and international trade. To reduce this problem, the collaborative efforts of education, apprehension, information sharing, and prosecution were used. The SARA model and the crime triangle, through collaborative problem solving helped to provide a methodology to reduce the problem of auto theft in both size and scope over a 10-year period. Additionally, centralizing the auto theft investigation function and implementing SCISS helped to further coordinate agency-wide information on the problem of auto theft, and to establish regular problem-solving strategy sessions.

A lesson learned from this decade-long effort is the complex nature of auto theft. No single strategy will reduce the problem. Multiple collaborative partnerships must be formed. The key is to recognize that many tactics and methods must be consistently applied over time to reduce the incidence of auto theft.

Chapter 6

Problem Solving for First Responders

J.D. Jamieson & Steve Griffith

Introduction

This chapter explores the problem of active shooter violence and suggests how first responder training might be employed as an effective response to such events. In so doing, we first take a look at why we believe the need for this training exists. Beyond the need for first responder police training that has been underscored by recent high-profile events, we next examine what we think officers might need to know to be better prepared in the future. The last part of this chapter presents a model that has been developed in Texas to address the problem of active shooter violence. While data currently are being collected to determine the utility of this training, we believe that the approach described here offers a systematic method that will prepare uniformed law enforcement personnel for dangerous situations that they may see more of in the future. Accordingly, this chapter is unique because rather than addressing a specific problem in any single jurisdiction, it addresses a general challenge that law enforcement agencies must face regarding training officers to be able to respond appropriately to the threat of a very serious problem that could occur in any jurisdiction at any time.

Background

The term *active shooter*, as it is used in the law enforcement community today, refers to enigmatic individuals who decide to kill other people around them and keep on killing until they are stopped. In the 1960s and 1970s, high-profile events like the shooting of 45 people by Charles Whitman on the University of Texas campus; the riots in Los Angeles, Philadelphia, and other cities; and the Black September terrorist attack at the Munich Olympics led to the development of specialized tactical teams, such as SWAT, to deliver the primary response by law enforcement to active shooter scenarios (Nichols, 2003.)

Through the 1980s and 1990s, tactical units became widely available, even though their response time to an active shooter event might be as long as two or three hours (Stockton, 2000.) At the same time, the role of the first responding patrol officers was reduced to containment of the event in a particular location, ensuring the safety of bystanders and victims who were able to escape the violence, and providing intelligence to the SWAT team when it arrived. With the tactical team system firmly in place, regular patrol officers pulled back into a support role because they still generally lacked the training and skills needed to effectively minimize harm and achieve closure in active shooter situations. Interestingly enough, field supervisors were generally unwilling or unable to apply any alternative to tactical unit deployment in active shooter events. Such an approach worked well for situations headed for lengthy standoffs between police personnel and a relatively patient shooter.

Unfortunately, active shooters can inflict significant harm during the time that elapses between the arrival of patrol and intervention by the tactical unit. This became painfully obvious in the Columbine High School tragedy in Littleton, Colorado, in April of 1999 (Tracey, 1999). In this tragic event, two shooters planned a massive attack on the people in the school and on the police officers they knew would respond. Bombs were planted in the school with the intent of collapsing an upper floor onto a crowded cafeteria below. More bombs were planted outside to explode in the presence of police responders, and a remote device was planted away from the school as a diversion. Fortunately, only the diversionary device detonated, and the shooters started their attack outside the school with firearms. Deputy Neil Gardner arrived at the scene at 11:24 A.M., about one minute after receiving the call from dispatch, and received fire from one of the shooters immediately. Deputy Gardner returned fire with a .45 caliber service weapon at a distance of 60 yards, and when the shooter retreated to the school, Gardner called for assistance and began assisting fleeing students to safety. In the next six minutes, five more officers arrived, and as they tried to establish perimeter containment, they received reports of as many as eight shooters, rooftop snipers, and suspects fleeing amid the escaping students, bombs, fire, and hostages. Some of the escaping victims were injured and needed help. Shooting continued inside the school. By 11:44 A.M. the containment perimeter was secured, and by 11:52 A.M. a SWAT team was assembled, organized, and authorized to enter the school. Additional SWAT and paramedic personnel received and returned fire at 12:02 P.M., and at 12:05 P.M. the last shots were heard from inside the school.

Additional ad hoc SWAT teams were deployed into the school, but all progress was slowed by the discovery of explosive devices. These threats were neutralized, the school was systematically secured, and no further harm occurred. At 3:30 P.M. SWAT personnel found the bodies of the shooters in the school library, dead by suicide. Fifteen people died in the school, including one teacher and the shooters, 24 others were critically wounded, and 160 were injured to a lesser degree.

Problem

It is apparent from recent events that public safety agencies typically are unprepared to immediately respond to calls involving active shooters or other potentially deadly circumstances that require a rapid intervention to avoid high loss of human life. The immediate problems encountered by first responders on the scene of situations involving active shooter violence typically require specialized abilities for officer safety and successful resolution of life-threatening situations. Unfortunately, few regular patrol officers ever receive the specialized training designed to minimize harm in deadly environments, even though these officers are often the first to arrive at events that subsequently turn violent.

First responder training should be designed to minimize the most important types of challenges encountered by patrol officers from the moment they receive a call to respond when active violence has occurred or is a possibility. The following discussion of problems faced by first responders is by no means exhaustive, but it does provide a basis for determining the types of training that would be most beneficial for patrol officers, perhaps from different agencies, who are the first to arrive at a scene of active violence.

Specialized SWAT-type units train and practice continually and thus arrive at an active scene with tactical teamwork skills in place. They can establish tactical goals and move into operation very quickly once on the scene. In contrast, patrol officers often lack fundamental knowledge of tactical team operations, thus making it difficult to form ad hoc tactical units of officers, especially if the first responders are from different agencies with different training practices or diverse standard operating procedures. More specifically, regular patrol officers often lack the basic skills necessary for safe, effective operations in hostile environments. They are often unfamiliar with small-team movement techniques and with dynamic entry and room-clearing techniques. Patrol officers generally are unfamiliar with specialized methods for operating in dark and low-light environments, and are often unfamiliar with covert searching techniques typically used by specialized tactical units in buildings and residential structures. Furthermore, patrol officers often are unfamiliar with intervention tactics commonly used in confrontations with active shooters and barricaded suspects.

Future challenges for police in the United States include the probability of increasing encounters with suspects armed with portable bombs and other atypical weaponry. While specialized units are usually trained to recognize these threats, patrol officers are unfamiliar with the operation of exotic or foreign weapons commonly available to potential active shooters and are often unable to identify improvised explosive devices such as those encountered at Columbine or commonly used by terrorists (Weiss & Dresser, 2002.)

Specialized units operate with intelligence components trained to develop and deliver accurate and pertinent information. First responders, however, receive initial information transmitted from dispatch that is often inaccurate, confusing, and conflicting (Siuru, 2003) and in turn often communicate back to dispatch from the scene in chaotic fashion. Getting initial information out to officers must be done quickly, but communications operators often work simultaneously with multiple callers and find it difficult to glean factual, new information from various callers without wasting time. Notification of the event to multiple agencies must be made, and thus keeping new information flowing to responding officers may be difficult (Wimberly, 2003.) Because of incomplete communication, patrol officers responding to a scene are often unable to anticipate the range of possibilities that might be encountered (Weiss & Dresser, 2002.)

Specialized tactical units are trained to use systematically developed information to form an accurate initial assessment of an active scene, establish tactical goals quickly, and formulate plans to achieve their goals. Patrol officers as first responders often lack the training necessary to assemble information, calculate resources available, and develop an effective, flexible plan of action while en route to an active shooter event. Information necessary to build an on-scene plan of action may be missing, and officers may not have key pieces of information that govern a tactical/negation versus an active response. As supervisors become involved in an event, communication of situation goals by commanders to first responders may prove difficult. Officers often are unable to leave a vital communication link behind to coordinate subsequent response. If a patrol officer enters a violent environment, communication about developing circumstances between the first responder and subsequent responders may be difficult. Clear communication between responding patrol officers often is difficult, and communicating across different agencies may also be difficult because of significant differences in operating procedures and training (Ake, 2003.) Finally, first responders rarely plan for an escalation or de-escalation of events as tactical units are trained to do.

Active shooter events are, of course, highly stressful occurrences as well. The wide range of physical and mental changes that individuals may experience under stress can have very negative, and even fatal, consequences. Members of specialized tactical units are trained to anticipate such involuntary reactions and neutralize their effects. Unfortunately, first responding patrol officers are not usually trained to compensate for the changes in physical motor abilities and cognitive ability that occur during high stress. In volatile environments, patrol officers may be unable to compensate for deterioration of fine motor skills or for visual and auditory perception distortion. They usually are not trained to deal with temporary memory loss or to recognize and accommodate time distortion effects. Patrol officers may not be aware that they might experience cognitive distortion effects such as detachment, dissociation, and distractive thinking, or that they might even experience temporary paralysis.

Tactical officers are trained to remain vigilant throughout an encounter, from the call for assistance and arrival at the scene to the ultimate transfer of command back to normal police jurisdiction. When an immediate threat is controlled by patrol officers, they may not anticipate continuing dangers or attend ongoing responsibilities (Garrison, 2003.) Officers may lack training in procedures for rescue and recovery of victims as well as in the care of injured persons. Following a violent encounter, patrol officers often forget to maintain control of the crime scene and protect evidence. Patrol officers often neglect to continue to "expect the unexpected," such as improvised explosive or incendiary devices or subsequent violence by additional suspects (Fuller, 1999.) Finally, officers may not be trained in procedures for the systematic transfer of command.

Problem-Solving Approach

In 2002 Sergeant Terry Nichols of the San Marcos, Texas, Police Department and the Hays County SWAT Unit; Steve Griffith, then chief of police of San Marcos; and colleagues in the Department of Criminal Justice at Texas State University considered the many advantages that would be associated with standardized first responder training for patrol officers in the United States. Nichols and his associates conceptualized what was to become the Advanced Law Enforcement Rapid Response Training (ALERRT) Center and, with Sergeant David Burns, also a SWAT leader and member of the Hays County Sheriff's Office, developed a model first responder training curriculum based on lessons learned from a history of active shooter incidents and other homicidal/suicidal acts of violence, their knowledge of tactical unit operations and training, and their close associations with experienced tactical officers in Texas and around the nation.

The ALERRT Center was established at Texas State University–San Marcos with funding from the U.S. Department of Justice and the State of Texas Governor's Office. The ALERRT mission is to deliver training assessed to be critically important for regular patrol officers who would typically be the first to arrive at violent situations. The ALERRT staff is working to establish a nationally standardized format for the training and a "train-the-trainer" delivery system to meet the needs of law enforcement agencies nationwide. While ALERRT conducts a range of advanced tactical refresher courses, the first responder course consists of the following subject areas:

- Communication, command, and control for active shooter situations

- Fundamentals of tactical team operations

- Small-team movement, formation, and communication

- Operations in low-light environments

- Active shooter intervention/barricaded shooter intervention

- Covert searching techniques

- Tactical building entry and room-clearing techniques

- Basic tactical firearms

- Mental preparedness/neutralizing the effects of survival stress reaction

The Delivery of ALERRT Training

To date, the ALERRT Center staff has conducted more than 20,000 contact hours of first responder training in 20 geographic areas across the United States. More than 1,000 ALERRT graduates carry enhanced first responder skills with them every day on patrol.

The *communication, command, and control* training for active shooter situations skills training prepares patrol officers to better process information coming from dispatchers who may be communicating with multiple excited callers simultaneously. Rapid assessment and contingency planning is covered, as is the preparation of communication lines to arriving commanders, officers, and tactical units.

The *fundamentals of tactical team operations* training prepares officers to form rapidly into tactical units with other responding officers, perhaps from other agencies, and achieve situational objectives with systematic teamwork. Rapid communication and commitment to tactical goals, along with team member roles and responsibilities, are emphasized.

The *small-team movement, formation, and communication* training prepares officers to organize into teams of two, three, four, or five officers and move to the objective as safely as possible in a hostile environment. Hand-signal communication, fields of responsibility, and safety precautions are taught to develop the ability to function effectively as a team member, particularly when team members are previously unknown to each other. Standardized communications, formations, and tactics are emphasized for rapid deployment by teams with diverse members.

Training for *operations in low-light environments* includes understanding and applying basic tactical lighting principles, the correct use of lighting equipment, and the use of low-light situations as an advantage in a dangerous confrontation. Students are trained to adapt quickly to changes in lighting and to understand how the dynamics and "mindset" of a confrontation change as the light conditions change. Students are trained to assess lighting conditions and to anticipate how they would be perceived by threats in darker or lighter areas. Communication with lighting tools is covered, as is the use of lighting tools to control and incapacitate suspects.

Active shooter intervention/barricaded shooter intervention training involves preparing officers for the possibility of exchanging fire with suspects. ALERRT employs a range of simulation technology, including "simunition" weapons for force-on-force exercises, along with live-fire exercises to give the students critical skills in shooting techniques while maximizing the use of cover and movement.

In addition, training in *covert searching techniques* equips the officer to safely and systematically locate and approach survivors or threats in hostile environments. Students learn to search through structures and other operational environments as a team.

Training in *dynamic entry and room clearing* equips the officer to use the elements of speed, surprise, and violent action to make an effective tactical entry into a potentially hostile structure or room. Students learn to systematically reduce threats and evaluate targets rapidly.

Basic *tactical firearms* instruction familiarizes the students with weapons commonly used by tactical teams and with the safe application of standard police weaponry in the stressful circumstances encountered by first responders. Students are trained to move and acquire cover during an engagement and to minimize exposure while stopping the threat. Training includes a close evaluation of the students' shooting skills by tactical firearms experts.

Finally, *mental preparedness* training prepares the officer to neutralize the effects of survival stress reaction. Officers are instructed in the causes of such abnormalities as tunnel vision, memory loss, time and hearing distortion, thoughts of detachment or dissociation, distracted thinking, or even temporary paralysis that may occur during highly stressful, threatening events. Students learn training techniques that minimize the effects of motor skill deterioration and other survival stress reactions.

Conclusion

In the 1960s, our problem was that regular patrol officers were not trained and organized to cope with dangerous active shooter environments. The response of developing tactical teams has been a good one. These units are effective and invaluable. The problem that remains in the present day, however, is that *active shooters often inflict considerable harm in the interval between the arrival of first responder patrol officers and the effective deployment of tactical teams*. Regular training for patrol officers that would equip them to operate effectively, at least to some degree, in the initial stages of an active shooter event could prevent significant harm (Nichols, 2003).

Perhaps the most important lesson we have learned from catastrophic tragedies such as have occurred at public schools, post offices, college campuses, government office buildings, and business establishments is that no environment in our country is completely immune from the possibility of active shooter violence. It can occur anywhere, anytime, and without any significant warning. Any police officer—veteran or rookie—may be called upon at a moment's notice to respond effectively and minimize harm in a dangerous circumstance. Standard training for police recruits in the United States generally does not include the development of skills necessary for effective performance when this happens (Nichols, 2003).

While traditional police problem solving tends to concentrate on persistent crime-related issues, many immediate problems encountered by first responders to critical events often involve not only the behavior of violent suspects but also that of police dispatchers, witnesses and victims, other police officers, remote command supervisors, and factors that continually affect the psychological and sensory status of the individual responding officers. Minimizing the harm that occurs in potentially deadly circumstances requires effective communication, thorough and flexible planning, and operational and mental readiness (Garner, 1998).

It appears that the role of patrol officers responding to critical events will again resemble, to some degree, their duties as they existed prior to the development of specialized tactical units. Although tactical units are immensely valuable and irreplaceable as a law enforcement resource, there will be increasing expectations for patrol officers to take some tactical action as they arrive on the scene of active violence. First responders can take effective, planned action and save lives. It is important that we intensify our efforts to provide patrol officers with the essential tactical skills and knowledge. Ideally, future tactical training for patrol officers will be increasingly standardized across the nation in order to allow the rapid formation of effective tactical teams composed of regular patrol officers when events call for such action. We do not know when or where the next Columbine, Oklahoma City, or World Trade Center catastrophe might occur. We can predict with some certainty, however, that such events *will* occur. As Les Poole notes in Chapter 14, failing to plan is planning to fail. The same is true regarding preparing first responders for active shooter violence. Failing to prepare is preparing to fail when these situations occur.

References

Ake, G. (2003). "First Responder Communication Across Jurisdictional Boundaries." *The Police Chief* 70(7):20.

Fuller, T.C. (1999). "Bomb Threat: A Primer for the First Responder." *FBI Law Enforcement Bulletin* 68(3):28-32.

Garner, G.W. (1998). "Before SWAT Arrives: Negotiation Skills for First Responders." *Police* 22(4):26.

Garrison, D., Jr. (2003). "Crime Scene Investigation as a Patrol Function." *Law & Order* 51(11):70.

Nichols, T. (2003). "Enhancing Training with Firearms Simulations." *Law & Order* 51(6):88.

Siuru, B. (2003). "Columbine Inspires New Technology for First Responders." *Law & Order* 51(6):128.

Stockton, D. (2000). "SWAT in Small Towns." *Law & Order* 48(3):75-79.

Tracey, D.J., and D.F. Buchanan (1999). "School Violence: Critical Incident Response for First Responders." *The Police Chief* 66(10): 94-97.

Weiss, J., and M. Dresser (2002). "Bomb Threat Recognition." *Law & Order* 50(1):75-80.

Wimberly, R. (2003). "High-Speed Notification." *Law & Order* 51(6):107.

Chapter 7

Preparing Supervisors for Effective Problem Solving

Timothy N. Oettmeier

Introduction

For the past several years, police executives have been challenged by Herman Goldstein's bold initiative of incorporating problem solving into their repertoire of thinking about and responding to various types of service demands. As attractive and enticing as problem solving may be, many police executives struggle with how to incorporate it within their agency. Despite the appearance of the concept being a straightforward one, there are significant issues executives should consider before "jumping in with both feet."

Clearly, the bulk of attention has been placed on trying to figure out how police officers can become effective problem solvers. One of the more pervasive debates is whether police officers can implement problem solving while remaining locked into the call-for-service response loop. How many times have we heard about the successful problem-solving escapades of officers whose sole responsibility was to work on a particular issue without the threat of being interrupted to run a call? Not all departments have the luxury of creating special problem-solving units, so the prospect of administering various types of problem-solving projects while simultaneously handling calls and other duties is a real dilemma.

Background

What tends to get lost in the pursuit of problem-solving utopia is a set of expectations it places on supervisors and managers. The simple fact is that problem solving leads sergeants and lieutenants to work harder.[1] And unless one of the basic tenets of human behavior has changed, that is not something people occupying those positions get very excited about. Does that mean it is pointless to proceed? Not at all—it just represents an additional obstacle that must be dealt with.

Problems and Solutions: What's In It for Me?

People who have rank within police organizations usually have tenure. Tenure is symptomatic of experience and, hopefully, wisdom. So when one begins to talk about problem-solving responsibilities to "experienced" sergeants and lieutenants, it is highly unlikely that one can pull the proverbial wool over their eyes. So the question "What's in it for me?" is a fair one that demands attention in the form of several answers.

First, officers get bored—some rather easily. The routine of police work becomes hypnotic, lulling officers into "intellectual complacency" and numbing their desire to be creative. Problem solving can serve as a motivator, providing officers with opportunities to demonstrate to themselves and their superiors that they can make a meaningful difference within their community.

Second, citizens are placing increasing demands for service on the police. As frustrations grow with individuals responsible for repeated acts of disorder, nuisance activities, or other more serious and persistent threats to the public's sense of safety and well-being in their neighborhoods, citizens expect action from the police. Because there are limited resources available to address these issues, along with other competing service demands, the police must become more creative in how they approach and perform their work. Problem solving serves as a catalyst that can encourage "innovative effectiveness."

Third, although problem solving is a challenge, it can serve as a motivating influence. Supervisors and managers need to be inspired just as much as officers do. Problem solving can ignite an intrinsic desire within a person to make a unique kind of contribution when addressing crime and disorder. One of the more interesting aspects of this concept is that a problem's nature and level of complexity poses different types of challenges for supervisors and managers. These challenges take the form of learning and applying new skills, extending managerial responsibilities, and becoming accountable for different types of results produced by the involved parties.

Finally, problem solving provides opportunities for sergeants and lieutenants to distinguish themselves from others within their respective ranks. The likelihood of this happening on a regular basis is linked, in part, to incentives within the organization. Transfer criteria for certain assignments, promotion criteria, and performance-based evaluations for pay can help stimulate interest to become involved even within the most reserved individual.

Personal Preparation: Before You Begin, Consider . . .

Being committed and motivated to incorporate problem solving within an officer's daily routine is not sufficient in and of itself. A sergeant or lieutenant's degree of success in supervising and managing problem-solving initiatives depends heavily on several other factors. These factors will have a direct bearing on the difficulty or ease with which problem solving can be supported by them and their superiors, and performed by their officers.

Educate Yourself. Sergeants and lieutenants should take time to learn all they can about the concept of problem solving. There is so much literature available now that all anyone has to do is read some of it. They should become familiar with organizational policies concerning their ability to free officers' time for problem solving. Sergeants and lieutenants should demonstrate a commitment to become familiar with the neighborhood leaders with whom their officers are likely to come into contact. They should make contacts with people in other community groups and organizations whose support may be needed to address specific types of problems. They should discuss with them what their officers will be attempting to do and that they may be contacted by them to ask for assistance.

Classifying Problems.[2] The old adage "one size fits all" has inhibited the business of policing for years. Care must be exercised to recognize that problems do have variability. "Simple" problems (e.g., repeated loud noise complaints about a neighborhood club) are often those that can be readily addressed by an officer, either in isolation or in conjunction with his or her partner. "Moderate" problems (e.g., crack house operations in a neighborhood) usually require the involvement of a team of people. The team can consist of a squad of officers led by a supervisor. It also could consist of a group of officers and citizens working together but addressing different attributes of a problem. "Complex" problems (i.e., handling mentally ill individuals) typically require collaboration between agencies. The ability to achieve success with these endeavors depends upon integrating decisions made by all personnel who are affected by or have some control over different facets of a complex problem and the corresponding solution. The point of acknowledging differences in the complexity among problems is this: as the sophistication of a problem increases, so does the amount of supervision and management needed to guide the effort toward a successful resolution. This has a direct bearing on the types of responsibility sergeants and lieutenants must exercise in order to support the efforts of their officers.

Firsthand Experience. It is important for sergeants and lieutenants to actually have some firsthand experience with problem solving beyond what may be gained from their readings. One reason this is crucial is because a supervisor or a manager must know what types of questions to ask and what types of answers to provide when helping an officer navigate his or her way through the process.[3] This *critical analysis skill* is imperative if one wishes to properly gauge how well officers are progressing in their efforts to address a problem. Experience also places one in the position of being able to reasonably anticipate what will transpire before it actually does and to develop contingency responses for unexpected occurrences.

Assessing Officers' Abilities. Even in its simplest form, problem solving can be quite a challenge. This is not to suggest that officers are not intelligent enough to handle problem-solving projects. It is more a reflection of having little motivation, being impatient, or displaying a cynical attitude, coupled with the fact that some officers have a weak problem-solving skills. Please keep this in mind; problem solving is not a single skill. It is a process that requires the use of several skills.[4] Thus, sergeants must be cognizant of which officers possess those skills and are willing to use them. Otherwise, sergeants are doomed to failure before they begin.

Analyze Operational Capacity. If all problems encountered by officers or brought to their attention by citizens were simple ones, the challenge of managing the problem-solving process would be much easier. However, because problems have varying degrees of complexity, it is imperative for sergeants and lieutenants to do a little operational homework before allowing officers to engage in the process.

First and foremost, they must examine deployment obligations. Years ago it was not uncommon to have officers deployed equally across three primary shifts. This was based on the belief that work demands were equal across time. We now know that is not the case. Today deployment is driven in large part by call distribution patterns and response times. If the volume of calls is high, more officers are needed to keep response times low. We know the nature of a call affects deployment because officers spend more time on "complicated" calls than simple calls. We also know that officers perform a variety of other tasks such as issuing tickets, conducting preliminary investigations, and writing reports. Time not dedicated to any of these responsibilities is generally referred to as "uncommitted time."

If supervisors expect officers to work on neighborhood problems, sufficient uncommitted time must be available for them to do so. If this is not possible, a decision must be made to release officers from these duties and allow them to address problems as their sole responsibility.[5] In either event, a commitment to problem solving has repercussions throughout the patrol force and the agency's ability to provide a full spectrum of services within the community. Sergeants and lieutenants need to recognize and be prepared to cope with these repercussions before they happen.

There will be times when officers are so caught up in the performance of day-to-day responsibilities that they do not look at the nature of their work from a problem-solving perspective. Officers know they have to respond to calls, they realize crime occurs in their assigned areas, and they acknowledge that citizens can easily become frustrated with traffic mobility. What they do not always have the time to do is sufficiently analyze calls, crime, or traffic trends or patterns. Sergeants and lieutenants can assume some responsibility to become informed about these trends. Upon doing so, they should see that this information is immediately and consistently shared with their officers as a way of directing their attention toward specific problems. It is a far more efficient use of resources to direct officers toward problems if they refuse or are reluctant to demonstrate the initiative of doing so themselves.[6] As much as we would prefer officers to be "self-directed," this type of officer represents an exception to the norm. Most officers need a little push from their sergeants before they will engage. So when they are ready, step forward and give them a gentle nudge.

Finally, sergeants and lieutenants should have a good sense of resource availability within their agency. That includes personnel they control and do not control within their department, as well as vehicles, equipment, overtime, and volunteers from their community. The amount and type of resources affects what type of work can be done, how long work can be sustained, and whether innovative approaches can be used to address different types of problems.

Becoming a Problem-Solving Supervisor: If You Really Want To Do Well . . .

In 1989 the Police Executive Research Forum (PERF) developed a list of characteristics demonstrated by effective problem-oriented supervisors. Review them carefully, because they provide considerable insight as to how sergeants (and indirectly, lieutenants) can enhance their success in working with their officers to become effective problem solvers.

1. Allow officers the freedom to experiment with new approaches.

2. Insist on good, accurate analysis of problems.

3. Grant flexibility in work schedules when requests are proper.

4. Allow officers to make most contacts directly, and pave the way when they are having trouble getting started.

5. Protect officers from pressures within the department to revert to traditional response methods.

6. Run interference for officers to secure resources, protect them from criticism, etc.

7. Know what problems officers are working on and whether the problem is real (i.e., properly understood).

8. Know your officers' assigned areas (i.e., beats) and important citizens in them, and expect them to know such information even better than you do.

9. Coach your officers through the process, provide advice, help them manage their time, and help them develop work plans.

10. Monitor officers' progress on work plans and make adjustments when needed; motivate them, slow them down, etc.

11. Support officers even if their tactics fail, as long as something useful is learned in the process and the tactic was well thought-out.

12. Manage problem-solving efforts over a long period; do not allow an effort to die because competing demands for time and attention sidetrack it.

13. Give credit to officers and let others know about their good work.

14. Allow officers to talk with visitors or at conferences about their work.

15. Identify new resources and contacts for officers and have them investigated.

16. Stress cooperation, coordination, and communication within their unit and with other units.

17. Coordinate efforts across shifts, beats, and outside units and agencies when appropriate.

18. Provide officers with examples of good problem solving so they know generally what is expected.

19. Provide more positive reinforcement for good work than negative for poor work.

20. Expect officers to account for their time and activities, while giving them a greater range of freedom.

A Few More Words about Accountability

Accountability is clearly the most critical function associated with supervising and managing problem-solving initiatives. In its simplest form, accountability represents a process of holding an individual responsible for his or her actions. In the context of problem solving, there are several points about accountability that are worthy of consideration.

An officer will come to his or her sergeant seeking authorization to address a problem. As the authorizing entity for the department, the sergeant should have a good understanding of what the problem is and whether the pursuit of a resolution is possible and practical. This becomes even more important as multiple officers submit different requests for authorization to their sergeant. An old Clint Eastwood cliché, "a man has got to know his limitations," certainly applies to this situation. It is one thing for a sergeant to freely grant authorization to demonstrate support and commitment to addressing a neighborhood problem. It is an entirely different matter to effectively demonstrate an ability to properly supervise multiple problem-solving initiatives while simultaneously being held accountable for the performance of all other services officers are expected to provide.

Once a problem-solving initiative has been authorized, it is incumbent upon a supervisor to review the officer's progress. This is usually accomplished by the officer providing documentation to his or her sergeant. What is important is not the amount of documentation submitted, but that an officer and supervisor regularly discuss what progress is being made in pursuit of a resolution. Just as an officer expects to account for his or her actions to the supervisor, the supervisor should also expect to be accountable for his or her actions to his or her superior.

If at all possible, supervisors should monitor portions of their officers' performance as they work to address a particular problem. For sergeants, that may mean accompanying an officer when he or she visits "guardians, controllers, and managers."[7] It could also mean simply listening while officers discuss options with their colleagues or citizens or observing the actual implementation of a tactic. Officers must realize that their supervisor's presence is not meant to be a form of interference. Conversely, supervisors must respect an officer's desire to demonstrate that they can perform their responsibilities effectively by knowing when it is proper to intervene or make casual observations.

Eventually, both sergeants and lieutenants are will be held accountable for the results achieved by their officers. This makes it important that there be a clear and concise meaning of the term "results." From a technical perspective, "results" should be associated with *outcomes* as opposed to *outputs*.

Unfortunately, in policing there is a long history of associating results with quantifiable outputs. Such outputs represent nothing more than activities performed. Typical examples include the number of calls handled, tickets issued, reports written, citizens met, meetings attended, and so on. Outcomes, on the other hand, represent the *effect* of having performed the activities. In other words, what was the cumulative effect of issuing certain types of tickets over a certain period at a particular location? What was the effect of attending meetings or conducting extensive discussions with a specific group of citizens? Goldstein has identified five degrees of effectiveness associated with problem solving, each of which represents an outcome. Even he claims that the most realistic outcome associated with problem solving is the goal of reducing the number of incidents that a problem creates and reducing the seriousness of those incidents.

Of course, measuring effectiveness is not nearly as easy as counting activities.[8] This is probably why we are so comfortable with outputs—they are just so easy to count. Sergeants and lieutenants should avoid this "activity trap." It is less important to count how many problems officers handled and more meaningful to describe links between how neighborhood problems were addressed and what effects occurred because of those efforts. Under the best-case scenario, we want to account for cause and effect. We want the investment of our resources to create a benefit within neighborhoods. We want to make a genuine difference with our problem-solving efforts.

Two other points worth mentioning with respect to accountability are the need to conduct debriefing sessions with officers and the need to report results up the chain of command. The purpose of the debriefing session is to evaluate what was done and why it was done, and to determine whether improvements could be made to increase the probability of success. It provides an avenue for officers to share their accomplishments and frustrations with their supervisor. It provides supervisors with a time to coach and counsel. It is an opportunity for both parties to learn from their failures and successes.

Sergeants and lieutenants should never assume that their superiors know what is occurring under their watch. Nor should it be expected that superiors have been informed of what has been accomplished by their personnel. The last thing a sergeant needs is for something to go awry and attract media attention before word can be sent to his or her superiors. In these instances, superiors get infuriated because they did not know and thus could not respond properly to media inquiries. If the superiors had known, they would have been in a much better position to explain an officer's actions and perhaps even describe why things did not go according to plan. Reporting progress and results up the chain of command is an essential part of the accountability process. It is equally important for sergeants to begin the process of informing their superiors as it is for superiors to generate inquiries down the chain of command.

Conclusion

The message in this chapter is not that problem solving is too complicated or requires too much work, but that it represents an opportunity for law enforcement officers to think and act differently as they go about the business of policing within their communities. It provides them with opportunities and challenges to become creative, reach out, and overcome some of the monotonous and mundane aspects of police work. The real beauty of this business is that as practitioners working with citizens, police officers can select projects they deem to be worthwhile. They know from their own experiences that each neighborhood within their respective communities has its own unique set of problems. Given that each neighborhood is a little bit different from others, it means there are plenty of problems to keep everyone challenged and occupied. All they have to do is step up and seize the opportunity to become involved and make a real difference.

Notes

1. For the purpose of this chapter, we are representing sergeants and lieutenants who are assigned to patrol operations.

2. An assumption is being made that agreement exists as to what actually constitutes a problem, otherwise this discussion is too premature.

3. This is a very significant point. Guiding the problem-solving process demands a skill set from sergeants and lieutenants that may be different than what they are accustomed to.

4. It is interesting that performance evaluation forms include "problem solving" as one of many criteria upon which to judge officer performance. This is an unfortunate oversight for officers, for it fails to capture the true effectiveness of their ability to perform the complete set of problem-solving skills.

5. Obviously, there are benefits and detriments to this decision, and such a discussion lies outside the scope of this chapter. But this discussion needs to occur within an agency because it has dramatic implications on how well the commitment to genuine problem solving will be accepted within the department, especially by those officers assigned to patrol operations.

6. This perspective assumes that the "scanning phase" of problem solving should *not* rest solely on the backs of police officers. The more knowledgeable a sergeant or lieutenant is about a problem, the easier it will be for them to manage the process and allocate and utilize their resources more efficiently. Yet, this is a delicate balance because we do not want officers to discard their responsibility of continuously scanning their environment in search of legitimate problems they can address.

7. These are the people who exert control over the different sides of the crime triangle.

8. Part of the fun, along with the growth and development opportunities problem solving provides, is determining how best to measure effectiveness. It requires a commitment to such things as reviewing data, interviewing participants and targets, conducting surveys, and documenting visible signs of progress. All of this need not be overly complicated nor should department personnel perform these tasks in isolation. One might be surprised by how many volunteers are willing to step up and help.

References

Goldstein, H. (1990). *Problem-Oriented Policing*. New York: McGraw-Hill.

Section III

Problem Solving with Community-Based Partnerships

Chapter 8

Problem Solving Emergent Gangs in Suburban Washington State: The Mountlake Terrace Neutral Zone-AmeriCorps Program*

David Mueller, Quint C. Thurman & Cary Heck

Introduction

Throughout the ages adults have complained that the world "is in the biggest mess it's ever been in" (Jensen & Rojek, 1998:5). In the United States, much of this anxiety is focused on high crime rates, and much of our crime problems are rightfully attributed to young people. Between January 1993 and January 1994, Americans' ranking of crime and violence as the nation's foremost problem jumped from 9 to 49 percent (Gallup, 1994). According to Chiricos (2002), this spike in public fear was a reaction to sensational media coverage about gangs and the spread of gang violence beyond the inner city and into respectable middle-class communities. This paper examines one approach to gang problems in a suburban area of Seattle.

Background

Data from the 1996 National Youth Gang Survey (NYGS) indicated that there were about 31,000 gangs operating in 4,800 U.S. cities nationwide. Overall, gang membership at the time was estimated at more than 846,000

*This chapter is adapted from an article that originally appeared in *Community Policing in a Rural Setting*, Second Edition, by Quint C. Thurman and Edmund F. McGarrell (eds.), copyright © 2003 by Anderson Publishing Co.

individuals, half of whom were under the age of 18 (OJJDP, 1999). Cities such as Los Angeles, Chicago, and New York have endured serious and entrenched gang problems for many decades. However, small suburban communities are not immune to this "big city" phenomenon. In fact, data from the NYGS indicate that gangs began to pose a problem in 1990 for suburban counties, in 1992 for small cities, and in 1993 for rural counties.

Most gang activity in the United States is concentrated in big cities. Seventy-four percent of law enforcement agencies responding to the 1996 NYGS reported an active gang presence in these jurisdictions. However, police agencies also reported the presence of gangs in 57 percent of suburban communities, 34 percent of small U.S. cities (e.g., populations between 2,500 and 25,000 citizens), and 25 percent of rural communities (Snyder & Sickmund, 1999:77-79). In an effort to demonstrate how communities were coping with their particular gang problems, researchers Spergel and Curry (1990) surveyed 254 criminal justice and community agencies in 45 cities nationwide. The findings of this study indicated that community responses to gangs could be categorized into four broad areas: community organization, social intervention, opportunities provision, and police suppression.

According to Spergel and Curry (1990), the community organization approach is designed to combat gang activity through interagency cooperation, coordination, and communication between community groups and organizations. This approach also stressed the importance of mobilizing citizens and school personnel to combat gang activity in public places. The social intervention approach was characterized as a broad community outreach initiative highlighting widespread use of social workers, intervention and prevention programs, and referral services to "change the values of youths in such a way as to make gang involvement less likely" (Spergel & Curry, 1990:296). The opportunities provision model, on the other hand, stressed the importance of providing at-risk youth with legitimate jobs, job training, and one-on-one educational services so as to draw them away from gang life. Finally, the suppression approach highlighted the use of law enforcement initiatives such as intelligence gathering, mass arrests, and special prosecution of gang leaders.

Spergel and Curry (1990) found that many communities (44%) adopted a strategy of suppression to "crack down" on gang violence, while others (31.5%) adopted the social intervention model. Few, however, adopted community organization (8.9%) and opportunities provision (4.8%) as strategies to deal with gang problems. Follow-up research conducted three years later asked many of these same agencies about the perceived effectiveness of their anti-gang initiatives (Spergel & Curry, 1993). Surprisingly, these findings indicated that the most commonly adopted strategies (e.g., suppression and social intervention) were perceived as relatively ineffective, whereas the least commonly adopted approaches (e.g., community organization and opportunities provision) were apparently the most effective, particularly in the cities where gangs had not become entrenched.

These findings have important implications for the current study insofar as they speak to the policy tug of war that was occurring in the city of Mountlake Terrace, Washington, in the early 1990s. Like many cities at the time, Mountlake Terrace witnessed a dramatic increase in juvenile arrests during the early 1990s. Conventional wisdom in the community was that hard-nosed police suppression tactics such as crackdowns and the implementation of a late-night juvenile curfew were needed. Those who advocated a more measured response were quickly dismissed. Critics pointed out that "hug-a-thug" programs would simply send the wrong message to gang-affiliated youth. Indeed, there is some truth to this criticism, because many community-based crime prevention programs fall victim to a common criticism: they sound good, feel good, look good, but don't *work* good (Palumbo et al., 1993).

Given the community's growing concerns, Mountlake Terrace Police Chief John Turner was under considerable public pressure to "do something" to reduce the growing threat of juvenile crime. However, Chief Turner, a seasoned police veteran, was not persuaded by the calls for a simplistic quick fix. Instead, he endorsed a more comprehensive preventive approach to the city's youth gang problem, one that looked eerily reminiscent of the much-maligned midnight basketball programs endorsed by the Clinton administration. Many of Chief Turner's contemporaries were baffled by his approach. Midnight basketball, they grumbled, was simply not "real" police work. Some even argued that his program would act as a "gang magnet," drawing in rival members from neighboring jurisdictions and resulting in even more problems. The following pages provide a brief description about Chief Turner's innovative approach and its resulting impact on youth crime in the city of Mountlake Terrace.

The Problem

The city of Mountlake Terrace, Washington, is a working-class suburb located several miles north of Seattle. Like other cities located near a large urban center, Mountlake Terrace has experienced its share of crime and disorder, but in the early 1990s city officials were struggling to cope with what appeared to be an unprecedented surge of serious juvenile crime. In the five-year period between 1988 and 1992, juvenile arrests within the city of Mountlake Terrace rose by an alarming 63 percent. Additionally, the rate of juvenile arrests for violent crimes statewide had virtually doubled since 1982, even though there were fewer juveniles in the 10-year-old to 17-year-old at-risk age group (GJJAC, 1992).

Mountlake Terrace's juvenile crime problems came to a head during the summer of 1990. On back-to-back weekends in August 1990, Mountlake Terrace firefighters responded to a rash of suspicious fires that destroyed several prominent businesses and private dwellings in and around the city's commercial district. As residents arrived to watch the fires rage in the early morning hours, it was difficult for them to ignore the presence of so many juveniles who also had gathered at the scene. What were these kids doing out at two o'clock in the morning, anyway? Shouldn't they be home in bed? Surely they were up to no good. And thus the speculation began: kids had probably started those fires. Though the evidence linking juveniles to the fires was circumstantial (and in time turned out to be false), the recent rise in juvenile-related crime helped to reinforce what community residents already "knew." Something had to be done.

Instead of overreacting to the problem by jumping on the "curfew bandwagon," Chief Turner opted to hold a series of public meetings to allow residents to first vent their frustrations and then assess the likely causes of the problem before exploring possible long-term solutions. As expected, most residents initially clamored for a citywide curfew. Others disagreed, arguing instead that a late-night curfew would address only the symptoms of juvenile crime rather than its underlying causes. What was needed was a more permanent, proactive and, if possible, nonpunitive solution.

Problem-Solving Approach

Over time, an idea took hold that perhaps a better way to curb juvenile delinquency would be to involve area youths in a sports-related program designed to keep them busy and off the streets on weekend nights, when problems seemed to be at their worst. But would a midnight basketball program really produce the outcomes that local residents were hoping for? After reviewing a number of alternative strategies in various cities around the nation, Turner and a group of concerned Mountlake Terrace stakeholders called the Community Action Resource Team (CART) established a collaborative, nontraditional crime prevention program called the Neutral Zone. As originally conceived, the Neutral Zone was created to: (1) reduce the likelihood of youth involvement, as victims or perpetrators, in crime or violence on Mountlake Terrace streets, specifically during the most active periods of the week; (2) make inroads into the city's youth culture in order to help prevent delinquent activity; (3) provide an arena where recreation and community services are available to high-risk youth during the most crucial hours; and (4) allow youth, community volunteers, police, and other helping professionals to work together in an effort to seek more positive outcomes for high-risk youth (CART, 1993).

Designed and implemented as a proactive, community-based response to the problem of youth crime, the Neutral Zone offers juvenile participants, ages 13 to 20, an alternative environment in which to more productively pass their time during the most crime-prone hours of the weekend, on Fridays and Saturdays from 10:00 P.M. to 2:00 A.M. (see Payton, 1977; Levine & McEwen, 1985). Over the past 10 years the Neutral Zone has evolved into a multifaceted, educational, and service-oriented outreach program that has substantially reduced juvenile crime in and around the Mountlake Terrace area (see Thurman, Giacomazzi, Reisig & Mueller, 1996; Thurman & Mueller, 2003).

Although the Neutral Zone program was originally conceived as a safe haven for street kids and an alternative for potential gang members, it grew in scope to include a wide range of prosocial youth activities. In addition to its late-night recreational component, the program also offered both hot and cold meals during regular operating hours. As the number of participants rose, Neutral Zone staff and volunteers became aware that many of the youths were in need of more regularized food and clothing services. Thus, charitable donations were solicited from private citizens and area businesses in an effort to establish a small food and clothing bank for the city's homeless and "throwaway" kids. Interestingly, this service, which was primarily intended to help area youths, also appeared to have benefited local merchants and the police department in unexpected ways. For example, by reducing the motivation for kids to steal food and clothing out of need, the food and clothing bank helped to reduce the number of petty crimes in the area such as shoplifting and theft from local merchants.

While not designed as a cure-all for the many problems that youths face during their teenage years, the Neutral Zone also began to offer a number of health-related programs designed to benefit adolescents, including Alcoholics Anonymous, Narcotics Anonymous, HIV/AIDS awareness, smoking cessation, and CPR/First Aid training. Community agencies, including Planned Parenthood and Pathways to Women, also offer program participants a number of social service seminars on topics such as birth control, anger management, assertiveness training, and other counseling services.

Functioning as a community outreach program, the Neutral Zone also served as a valuable resource for police intelligence on crimes committed by (and against) area street youths. Working to establish ties between street youths and the police, the program also made it easier for the police to influence juvenile behavior through positive, prosocial interaction. And while it is difficult to know with certainty what the long-term benefits of the Neutral Zone would be on area youth, the police, and the community, responses over the past five years were extremely positive (see Thurman, Burton, Mueller & Heck, 1996).

Results

Chief Turner, a strong proponent of community policing, anticipated several positive outcomes for his community by taking the preventive route to crime over a more reactive one. First, he believed that youth would be attracted to a late-night recreational program that offered them interesting and engaging opportunities to participate in productive activities. The Neutral Zone, he believed, would act as a form of "voluntary incapacitation" by luring area youth into a supportive and controlled environment where activities and supervision could be effectively monitored. Additionally, Turner argued, the program could help to cut down on the number of opportunities for youth to become either perpetrators or victims of criminal violence. In short, by involving area youth in structured, prosocial activities, the Neutral Zone could reduce the rates of both juvenile crime and victimization by simply offering the targeted group a more productive way to spend their free time during the late-night hours.

An external evaluation of the Neutral Zone in 1994 documented that approximately 150 to 200 youths attended the program each weekend night (Thurman et al., 1994). Subsequent investigation of the program found that when the Neutral Zone was closed for repairs in the last week of July and the first week of August, 1994, police calls for service in the city increased almost 30 percent (Thurman, Giacomazzi, Reisig & Mueller, 1996:290). Additionally, a story that ran in the *Seattle Times* (DeLeon, 1996) reported that graffiti in and around the Mountlake Terrace area had dropped from 85 incidents in 1994 to 28 in 1995, and gang-related crimes dropped from 135 incidents to 93 over the same period.

A 1996 performance audit of an expanded version of the Neutral Zone (with assistance from AmeriCorps, discussed below) found that the program was making significant strides toward increasing its overall impact on area youth. For example, the addition of program services ranging from tutoring and homework assistance to mentoring classes for seventh- and eighth-grade latchkey kids not only appears to be keeping them busy but seems to be making a real contribution in terms of preparing these individuals for life after adolescence (Thurman, Burton, Mueller & Heck, 1996).

Cost-Sharing and Collaboration

In order to minimize initial startup costs, Chief Turner and CART established the Neutral Zone program in a local elementary school in a residential area of Mountlake Terrace. Although the building itself could be used free of charge, concerns were raised about possible litigation costs if someone were to be hurt while attending the program. To ward off this possibility, Chief Turner and CART successfully petitioned state legislators to change the wording of existing laws to expand liability insurance to cover program participants.

The Neutral Zone originally was supported by charitable donations from individual and corporate sponsors. As the program grew and the newness wore off, the Neutral Zone was faced with the need to cultivate more and longer-term sources of funding. Although fund-raising efforts proved relatively successful, program administrators soon learned that alternative sources of funding at both the state and local levels were not available except for the more punitive suppression tactics discussed above. These funds were not pursued, however, because they did not further the program's ultimate goal of nonpunitive crime prevention.

In an effort to distance the program from the unpopular label of "midnight basketball program," Neutral Zone administrators applied for funding through the AmeriCorps program. At the time, AmeriCorps was a relatively new and innovative program implemented under the National Service Act and signed into law by President Clinton in September 1993. Seeing this as an opportunity to expand their present services, coverage, and capabilities, particularly in the area of education and community service, the Neutral Zone was awarded a $236,000 grant to continue its operations in January 1995. This new infusion of capital helped to support five AmeriCorps team leaders and 30 part-time assistants, although the late-night recreation program continues to operate on a $150,000 budget with funds provided primarily from regional charities and local businesses.

Aside from its success as a nonpunitive youth crime prevention program, Neutral Zone participants and volunteers alike appear to glean a number of useful skills (e.g., education, job skill training, anger management, assertiveness training) that are assumed, in the long run, to make an important difference in the lives of troubled teenagers. Prompted in large part by Chief Turner's vision, the Neutral Zone has become an excellent example of police-community problem solving. Beyond that, the adaptability and persistence of the Neutral Zone has sowed the seeds for its continued financial success, despite the usual problems that have a tendency to wear such programs down.

Conclusion

Juvenile delinquency is a complex social problem that has the potential to outpace limited police resources while further straining community relations between teachers, parents, businesses, and public service agencies. However, as the Neutral Zone story suggests, youth crime problems can be addressed and the damage reduced if both law enforcement and community members are willing to work to solve problems cooperatively. The early success of the Neutral Zone can be attributed to the collaborative and community-based nature of the program. However, its continued success will likely depend upon its ability to adapt and to meet the changing needs of its clientele. Many rural and suburban communities are in a particularly suitable position to implement similar interventions. Given the persistent nature of juvenile delinquency and the apparent need for proactive police problem-solving methods, community-building ventures such as the one described here offer promising solutions for challenging crime problems. However, as the term implies, "community building" must be a community effort. Toward that end, the Neutral Zone serves as a model that other jurisdictions can use to create their own police-community problem-solving teams.

References

Chiricos, T. (2002). "The Media, Moral Panics and the Politics of Crime Control." In G. Cole, M. Gertz, and A. Bunger (eds.), *The Criminal Justice System: Politics and Policies*, Eighth Edition. Belmont, CA: Wadsworth/Thomson Learning.

Community Action Resource Team (November 1993). *The Neutral Zone: A Non-Traditional Gang/Crime Prevention, Late Night Program for High-Risk Kids.* Mountlake Terrace, WA: Mountlake Terrace Police Department.

DeLeon, F.M. (1996). " 'Neutral Zone' A Big Winner—Mountlake Terrace's Teen Program Draws Credit for Cutting Crime Rate, Giving Youths Positive Things To Do." *Seattle Times* April 8:A1.

Gallup, G. (February 1994). *The Gallup Poll, No. 341.* Wilmington, DE: Scholarly Resources, Inc.

Governor's Juvenile Justice Advisory Committee (1992). *Juvenile Justice Report.* Olympia, WA: Department of Social and Health Services.

Jensen, G.F., and D.G. Rojek (1998). *Delinquency and Youth Crime,* Third Edition. Prospect Heights, IL: Waveland Press.

Office of Juvenile Justice and Delinquency Prevention (July 1999). *1996 National Youth Gang Survey.* NCJ 173964. Washington, DC: Office of Juvenile Justice and Delinquency Prevention. Data retrieved February 24, 2004, from OJJDP Web site: http://www.ojjdp. ncjrs.org/pubs/96natyouthgangsrvy/

Levine, M.J., and J.T McEwen (1985). *Patrol Deployment.* Report # J-LEAA-011-81. Washington, DC: National Institute of Justice.

Payton, G.T. (1977). *Patrol Procedure.* Los Angeles, CA: Legal Books Corporation.

Palumbo, D.J., R. Eskay, and M.A. Hallett (1993). "Do Gang Prevention Strategies Actually Reduce Crime?" *Journal of Gang Research* 1(4):1-10.

Snyder, H.N., and M. Sickmund (September 1999). *Juvenile Offenders and Victims: 1999 National Report.* Washington DC: Office of Juvenile Justice and Delinquency Prevention.

Spergel, I., and G.D. Curry (1990). "Strategies and Perceived Agency Effectiveness in Dealing with the Youth Gang Problem." In C. Huff (ed.), *Gangs in America.* Newbury Park, CA: Sage Publications.

Spergel, I., and G.D. Curry (1993). "The National Youth Gang Survey: A Research and Development Process." In A. Goldstein and C. Huff (eds.), *The Gang Intervention Handbook.* Champaign, IL: Research Press.

Thurman, Q.C., V.S. Burton Jr., D.G. Mueller, and C. Heck (1996). *A Performance Audit of the Neutral Zone-Americorps Peer Assistance and Development Program.* Pullman, WA: Northwest Evaluation Research Institute.

Thurman, Q.C., A.L. Giacomazzi, M.D. Reisig, and D.G. Mueller (1996). "Community-Based Gang Prevention and Intervention: An Evaluation of The Neutral Zone." *Crime and Delinquency* 42:279-295.

Thurman, Q.C., A.L. Giacomazzi, and M.D. Reisig (1994). *A Process Evaluation of the Mountlake Terrace Neutral Zone Gang Intervention Program.* Spokane, WA: Washington State Institute for Community-Oriented Policing.

Thurman, Q.C., and D.G. Mueller (2003). "Beyond Curfews and Crackdowns: An Overview of the Mountlake Terrace Neutral Zone-AmeriCorps Program." In S. Decker (ed.), *Policing Gangs and Youth Violence.* Belmont, CA: Wadsworth/Thomson Learning.

Chapter 9

Problem Solving Prostitution in a Problem Neighborhood*

D. Kim Rossmo & Doug Fisher

Introduction

During the past decade, police departments have suffered the simultaneous impacts of increasing service demands and shrinking resource availability. Cutbacks in social, psychological, and educational services, and an increasing crime rate, combined with governmental fiscal restraint have resulted in many more pressures being placed on the police—the agencies of last resort. Managers have strived to maximize the efficiency and effectiveness of police organizations in efforts to meet the new and often conflicting demands of communities.

Prioritizing calls and reducing services to the public have been the inevitable outcomes of such processes. As a result, the police have been increasingly forced to respond to their mandate in a reactive or incident-driven fashion. This traditional reactive approach suffers, however, from the problem of limited impact. Such "fire brigade" policing is not preventive in nature, and despite the best efforts of most police departments, service demands tend to keep rising. What is needed is a different, more proactive approach (Couper & Lobitz, 1991; Kelling & Moore, 1988). This chapter illustrates how problem solving was applied in a problem neighborhood to address prostitution and related social issues that had become a major public safety challenge.

*Source: Adapted from *RCMP Gazette*, "Problem-Oriented Policing in Vancouver" issue, articled titled "Problem-Oriented Policing: A Co-Operative Approach in Mount Pleasant, Vancouver" by Kim Rossmo and Doug Fisher, pp. 1-11, Vol. 55 No. 1 (1993). Reproduced with the permission of the Minister of Public Works and Government Services Canada (2004).

Background

Mount Pleasant is an inner-city neighborhood of Vancouver, British Columbia, with a variety of long-term social problems (City of Vancouver Planning Department, 1987; Douglas, 1986). Years of disappointment and compromise, external control by business interests, and conflict between industrial and residential interests has resulted, however, in the formation of a variety of community activist groups. More than once, Mount Pleasant residents have marched on city hall. In the mid-1980s, against this background of neglect, the outcome of two legal decisions resulted in the largest explosion of protests ever seen in the area.

In 1978 the Supreme Court of Canada decided that the definition of soliciting meant "pressing and persistent," and effectively neutered prostitution enforcement. In response to numerous complaints from the citizens in the West End of Vancouver, a high-rise residential area containing the infamous red-light strip of Davie Street, the British Columbia attorney general in 1984 obtained a civil injunction that moved all the prostitutes out of the area. Unfortunately, a good many of them started working along Broadway Avenue, which ran through the residential part of Mount Pleasant. The problem had merely been displaced, and suddenly Mount Pleasant had been handed a vexing new social problem.

The neighborhood became increasingly concerned with the new social problems they had literally inherited overnight. The street people and activities created a rising fear of crime—a fear fed by several sensationalistic news stories, some based in fact, some based in paranoia. Certain alleys and underground parking lots, many within a block of a local elementary school, became repositories for used condoms, needles, and worse. Traffic and noise increased during the late night hours as customers and window shoppers cruised the streets and back lanes checking out the prostitutes. Those who owned buildings in the area grew concerned about the possibility of falling property values. Mount Pleasant had long put up with several social problems, but this latest development acted as a catalyst for a community that had reached its saturation point.

Residents responded with letter-writing campaigns; sleep-ins at city hall; confrontational citizen action groups; street harassment tactics against prostitutes, pimps, and customers, and a sensationalistic media campaign. As a result of this and similar pressures from other antiprostitution groups in Canada's major metropolitan areas, the federal government introduced legislation, effective December 1985, that made it illegal to communicate in a public place for the purpose of selling or buying sex. After a period of initial abatement, however, the problem grew to its previous levels, and it soon became apparent that the new criminal law was largely ineffective (Rossmo & Routledge, 1990).

This resulted in certain community groups putting pressure on the police and on all levels of politicians in an effort to solve neighborhood problems involving prostitution and related activities. The situation was exacerbated by some politicians who began using inaccurate statistics to display dramatic and frightening increases in the crime rate of Mount Pleasant, concurrent with the start of the prostitution problem. Local newspapers ran stories referring to the neighborhood as "Mount Pleasant, the Bronx."

Problem-Solving Approach

In response to the problems in the community and the lack of communication between the police and the neighborhood, the Vancouver Police Department created the Mount Pleasant Liaison Team (MPLT) in December 1986. Concurrently, the Mount Pleasant Police Liaison Committee was formed, its members coming from the community, activist, and neighborhood groups, business organizations, other professional agencies, and a variety of interest groups.

One of the first tasks of the MPLT involved a detailed analysis of crime and social problems in Mount Pleasant, the results of which were shared with the committee and the public. Both a comparative inter-neighborhood evaluation and a historical analysis were conducted. The results of this research were in stark contrast to the image portrayed in the media and by certain politicians. The crime rate in Mount Pleasant was a matter for concern but definitely not for panic: the per capita recorded crime rate was approximately 30 percent higher than the Vancouver city average but consistent with other inner-city neighborhoods. The service-call load in the team area was the highest in the city, but then so was the authorized police strength.

No connection was found between reported crime rates and prostitution counts, the latter obtained from research conducted by Professor John Lowman of Simon Fraser University (1984, 1989). In fact, there was some suggestion that commercial crimes dropped on those streets that had turned into prostitution strips, probably due to the increased surveillance generated from additional traffic and police patrols.

Census variables such as percentage of population on welfare, mean annual income, proportion of rental units, and average length of residency all pointed to a low-income, transient population with few roots in the community (Vancouver Local Areas, 1985). It became clear that developing a stronger sense of community and reducing the fear of crime in Mount Pleasant were critical issues for neighborhood redevelopment.

Contacts were built with social service agencies, local businesses, community groups, and the media. This communication provided new sources of information and helped overcome group hostilities. When the MPLT first began, certain community groups refused to even talk to the police, blaming them for the various social problems that existed in the area. Open houses were held by the police and city planners to help bring a sense of small-town policing to an inner urban neighborhood of a large city.

It was one of the original principles of the MPLT that its members would retain a street presence and not become isolated in meetings or offices. Members were involved in handling calls, checking people, and undertaking long-term enforcement projects that could not be attempted by a patrol officer constrained by the demands of the police radio. The MPLT strived to serve as a resource to the officers in patrol. Consequently, long-term situations and problems not amenable to quick solutions were often referred to the MPLT for followup. Extra efforts to communicate with other patrol constables were made through shift flexibility, personal connections, and time commitments.

MPLT projects were often conducted with the assistance of other agencies: the city licensing and permits department, the health department, Revenue Canada special investigators, the Vancouver Integrated Intelligence Unit, local area and social planners, the bylaw prosecutor, the city legal department, the Ministry of Social Services and Housing, the School of Criminology at Simon Fraser University, immigration enforcement officers, and U.S. law enforcement agencies.

Results

Problem Apartment Buildings

The first MPLT projects centered on problem apartment buildings, the source of complaints of heavy prostitution and drug activity, attendant disturbances, paid-off building managers, and a history of police non-response. The Canadian Criminal Code contains sections dealing with bawdy houses, but their enforcement in "hostile" apartment buildings can be very difficult.

The MPLT attacked this problem by investigating and locating the person who owned the property. A personal visit would be paid by the police to this party, who often had never seen the buildings he or she owned and usually had absolutely no idea what activities were going on there. The problem would be explained by the MPLT to the owner and often in just a few days the conspiring apartment manager would be fired and the problem tenants evicted. In the few cases where there was a reluctance to cooperate, pressure was brought to bear by the licencing and permits department, the health department, and even the media. In some instances, the use of the special investigators at Revenue Canada proved to be very helpful.

Problem Bars

Many complaints from the neighborhood revolved around a local bar that was popular with the criminal element. Drug trafficking, merchandising of stolen property, public consumption of liquor, fights, impaired drivers, disturbances, and noise complaints were repeatedly reported to the police. Additionally, patrol officers noticed that a significant proportion of the calls they attended after 2:00 A.M. involved persons who had been drinking in this particular licenced premise.

Heavy police patrols and bar checks put pressure on the bar, and the owner of the hotel, worried about sanctions from the provincial liquor board, cooperated fully with the police. New management was brought in, increased security patrols were implemented, and tighter door admittance standards were instituted. Another effective tactic involved the alteration of the bar's closing practices. Previously, admittance and departure was through a door that led onto a quiet, residential side street. Patrons, drinking off-sale beer, would party and fight on the street and in the parking lot after leaving the bar. Unfortunately, this was during one of the busiest police call-load periods, and it was difficult to muster the police presence necessary to move the patrons along.

The management of the bar, in consultation with the police, blocked off this door at last call and forced departing patrons to use a back exit that led onto a busy arterial route. This accomplished several goals, including the reduction of noise on the residential streets; faster access to taxicabs, leading to quicker departures; increased exposure to passing witnesses and police patrols; and the destruction of the post-closing ambiance.

The single most effective change, however, was totally unanticipated. The provincial government liquor branch cut back the off-sales hours from 2:30 A.M. to 11:00 P.M. Most bars had a last call for liquor at 2:00 A.M. and everyone was required to be out by 2:30 A.M. Departing patrons would pick up cases of beer for further drinking outside or at "after-hours parties." There was an obvious connection between intoxicated parties obtaining liquor at 2:30 A.M. for further drinking and subsequent criminal acts and police calls for service.

By preventing those who wished to stay in the bars after 11:00 P.M. from purchasing off-sales (such liquor must be immediately taken out of the licenced premises), closing-time problems and spontaneous after-hours parties were significantly reduced. The local hotel association aggressively lobbied against this cutback in off-sales hours, but the reduction in crime statistics and specially prepared police reports, strongly supportive of the staggered hours, helped make the change permanent.

Another local nightclub, with a history of poor performance that had resulted in the previous cancellation of its liquor licence, attempted to reopen its doors with an increased seating capacity. Meetings were held between the new club owners and apprehensive community members, city planners, neighborhood organizers, and police representatives. Concerns were aired and a variety of structural changes in the nightclub building were implemented to address the problems. A thorough investigation into the business history of the nightclub, and a financial analysis of the companies currently behind it, uncovered certain information that convinced the liquor board not to grant the increase in the seating capacity of the licence. As a result, upon reopening, the club caused very few problems for the community and the police.

Juvenile Prostitution

Juvenile prostitution was one of the more critical issues that evolved from the overall prostitution situation in Mount Pleasant. Beyond the negative impact on the community, the social issue of prostitution raises concerns about child sexual and physical abuse and pedophilia. The majority of prostitutes start their careers as teenagers, and at any given time Vancouver has approximately 300 juvenile prostitutes who work the street.

The MPLT became the police department's representatives on the Inter-Ministerial Street Children's Committee (IMSCC), a multiagency policy recommendation and organizational advocacy group composed of representatives from social services, mental health, probation, education, social planning, health, and the police. The Street Children's Committee has been involved in a variety of projects, one of the more interesting being a subgroup task force that focused on the ten "worst" juvenile street prostitutes.

All agencies involved first shared their information on the targets and then cooperative strategies were developed based on the more comprehensive pictures of the subjects. The targeted juveniles were then contacted, usually by social service, police, or probation workers, and intensive intervention strategies implemented by all agencies. During the six months of the project it was found that such a problem-oriented approach was successful in removing a significant number of the juvenile prostitutes from the street.

By comparison with other programs, this approach was not only highly effective but also manpower-intensive and very expensive. One of the spin-offs from the project was the development of a "new" source of information. The MPLT began to receive valuable and timely intelligence from group home workers and social workers. Many of the street children would talk about the activities of their adult street associates. With the new inter-agency cooperation this information was now passed on to the police. One example concerned an escapee who was recaptured in a run-down motel, with the assistance of the Burnaby Detachment of the Royal Canadian Mounted Police (RCMP). This criminal was eventually deported to the United States to face armed robbery charges.

Hot Spots—Locations with High Police Call Loads

Upon hearing of the new liaison team, residents in one high-crime section of Mount Pleasant voiced complaints over a certain apartment building that seemed to serve as a focus for a variety of criminal activities. Noise complaints, disturbances, prostitutes coming and going, street fights, and open drug dealing created an environment of fear for other citizens in the immediate area. A murdered prostitute's body was dumped in the backyard of the apartment building and was not discovered—or at least not reported—for several days.

Meetings were held with managers and tenants from the surrounding buildings, and their complaints were carefully recorded. At the request of the police, several people agreed to keep logs of the dates, times, and pertinent details of all the problems they observed. In the meantime, the MPLT conducted an extensive geographic analysis of the police calls in that particular corner of Mount Pleasant.

The whole area was commonly regarded by the police and residents as a locality with high rates of crime; the research results, however, showed a different picture. The block on which the problem apartment building was situated was a hot spot, with a police call load of more than 100 times that of the surrounding area. If this particular location was factored out of the calculations, the immediate neighborhood actually had a moderate to low level of criminal activity. Furthermore, it appeared that the majority of the problems were connected with the third floor of the apartment building. In this particular case, however, the owner was not initially cooperative.

The assistance of other city departments was requested, and after their preliminary investigations strategies were developed in consultation with members of the City Legal Department. The owner was requested to attend a meeting in the office of the Director of Permits and Licences to explain why a show cause hearing should not be held to determine if his business licence to operate an apartment building should be revoked. Also in attendance were building inspectors, health inspectors, representatives of the police department, and members of the planning department representing that particular local area.

The owner's assertion that he had adequate on-site management was destroyed by a subsequent walk through the building with the MPLT. Every single apartment door was knocked on, and the owner was shocked to learn that there were no records and no background checks for a majority of the people who lived there. At one point, the police had to physically restrain a tenant who wanted to attack the owner over conditions inside the building.

This unsettling inspection (and the threat of the loss of his business licence) altered the attitude of the owner, who, with advice from the MPLT, brought in new on-site apartment managers and tenant screening procedures. The team police officers gave the apartment and the immediate surrounding area special attention, often walking a beat through the hallways, stairwells, and foyers of the building. A "zone of zero tolerance" was established in the block for any criminal infraction or traffic violation, and this fact was made very clear to those with whom the police dealt. The other neighbors continued to watch outside activities and were encouraged to call the police for any sort of problem.

These combined efforts resulted in a drastic and permanent reduction in the problems associated with the building. It would be incorrect to assume that the offenders had become rehabilitated—most of them just moved out and new ones were not allowed in. Even though displacement had occurred, what was important was the fact that the potentiation effect had been eliminated.

What this means is simply that the total is often greater than the sum of the parts: when the number of criminals in a certain geographic area reach a certain point, they develop support networks, become bold, and start to control things. Criminal acts are committed with ease, more openly and more often, while the fear of crime increases for the other citizens in the area. By destroying this effect and scattering the offenders, the area and streets were taken back for the law-abiding residents of the neighborhood.

Creation of the Prostitution Task Force

While the MPLT focused on community liaison and specific problem targets, the critical issue of street prostitution remained. The message from the community was still: "Move the prostitutes out of our residential neighborhoods!" To help address the difficult task of controlling street prostitution, the first Prostitution Task Force was formed in 1986 (Fisher, 1989). Every summer, the most active period for street prostitution, patrol squads in the area would donate a total of seven to ten personnel for the Task Force.

Although the general mandate of controlling prostitution would remain constant, the method of accomplishing this goal would change from year to year. Some summers the Prostitution Task Force was used as an intelligence-gathering service. In other years, pressure would be put on either the customers or the prostitutes. Research had shown that while vice enforcement of the new soliciting law had limited impact, aggressive patrol strategies could be successful in displacing prostitution.

Several specific tactics proved to be effective in moving the prostitutes. A high-profile, aggressive patrol stance was adopted from the beginning. All officers worked in uniform and drove marked patrol cars. Extra marked cars were left parked at corners of high prostitution activity, in effect "doubling" the police presence. The strip became a zone of zero tolerance with heavy bylaw and Motor Vehicle Act enforcement and both the general public and the street regulars were apprised of this fact. Bylaw tickets were "batched" and sent directly to the city prosecutor for rapid processing. The task force would then serve the resulting summonses on the street regulars.

All traffic stops and person checks were done with the overhead emergency lights flashing. This served three purposes: (1) it stopped prostitutes from working the area around the check; (2) it scared off any potential customer traffic; and (3) perhaps most important, it let the residents know the police were attacking the prostitution problem. This tactic did not go unnoticed. With every high-profile stop momentum was gained, and soon citizens started to realize that when they complained about a prostitute, the police would respond. Community meetings were attended to explain what the police department was trying to do. A working relationship was attained with citizens living near "hot spots" who were encouraged to watch, collect information, and to phone the Task Force office.

All prostitution checks were recorded (1,138 in 1989 alone) and the data entered by the Patrol South Intelligence Unit in a specially designed computer program. This comprehensive and up-to-date information proved to be very useful in undercover operations that intensively targeted those prostitutes who continued to work residential areas. The resulting soliciting charges included accused background sheets that listed the details of previous times the prostitute had been checked in that area, and evidence that the accused had repeatedly been told to stop working residential districts. Based on such information the accused prostitute would not be released under the provisions of the Bail Reform Act, and Crown Counsel would invariably be granted the requested "no go" bail area restriction. This approach was very successful in leading most of the prostitutes to plead guilty in order to speed up the expiration of their area restrictions.

The Prostitution Task Force also began to target the growing number of drug dealers in the area. Several cocaine "shooting galleries" had been established, and a strong drug connection was found to exist between these locations and the prostitution trade. Dealers were constantly checked and arrested if possible, or else told to move on. Several operations, with the assistance of certain community members, were conducted on the shooting galleries, and numerous arrests were made.

Along with the constant attention by the Task Force, a combined RCMP/Vancouver Police Department undercover operation, "Street Wise," took place in 1989. By mid-summer that year the Task Force had arrested several drug dealers (primarily involved in cocaine trafficking) and had closed down all the strip's shooting galleries. These actions, combined with a changing street population, resulted in the great majority of the drug scene leaving the Mount Pleasant area. In the spring of 1990, management decided to continue the Task Force on a permanent basis, both to maintain pressure on the prostitutes and to work on other area problems as they arose.

Conclusion

By 1991 the street characteristics of Mount Pleasant had radically changed. Almost every prostitute had been moved out of the residential areas and most of the known drug houses shut down. Communication lines with the community had been reopened, and neighborhood involvement significantly developed. The main political concerns had been addressed, and the Mount Pleasant citizens once again acknowledged their support of their police department. Maintenance of the street problems became the responsibility of modified Task Force teams and the general patrol officers.

By involving the community and other professional groups, and by working with realistic expectations, concrete goals were met and certain pressing problems solved. The combined efforts of all members of the community produced an impact impossible for single groups alone to achieve. Such results are encouraging for the future use of problem-oriented policing approaches in difficult situations that have been intractable to traditional policing methods (Goldstein, 1990; Spelman & Eck, 1987).

None of this would have been possible without the strong support of management. The flexibility and autonomy granted to the Mount Pleasant Liaison Team and the Prostitution Task Force allowed their projects to be accomplished in a timely and effective manner. The cooperation and assistance of other patrol constables and the area crime prevention officers was also invaluable in the accomplishment of the problem-solving goals.

References

City of Vancouver Planning Department and Vancouver Museum (1987). *Mt. Pleasant: A Walking Tour Through History*. Vancouver: Author.

Couper, D. C., and S. Lobitz (1991). "The Customer Is Always Right." *The Police Chief* (May):17-23.

Douglas, C. (1986). *Mount Pleasant: Brewery Creek*. Vancouver: Brewery Creek Urban Committee.

Eck, J.E., and W. Spelman (1987). *Problem-Oriented Policing* (National Institute of Justice Publication). Washington, DC: U.S. Government Printing Office.

Fisher, D.K. (1989). *1989 Prostitution Task Force Final Report*. Unpublished report. Vancouver: Vancouver Police Department.

Goldstein, H. (1990). *Problem-Oriented Policing*. New York: McGraw-Hill Publishing.

Kelling, G.L., and M.H. Moore (1988). *The Evolving Strategy of Policing* (Perspectives on Policing, No. 4, BJS Publication No. NCJ-114213). Washington, DC: U.S. Government Printing Office.

Lowman, J. (1984). *Vancouver Field Study of Prostitution: Research Notes*. Ottawa: Department of Justice, Programs and Research Branch.

_____ (1989). *Street Prostitution: Assessing the Impact of the Law, Vancouver*. Ottawa: Department of Justice.

Mount Pleasant Citizens Planning Committee (1987). *Community Development Plan for Mount Pleasant*. Vancouver: City of Vancouver Planning Department.

Rossmo, D.K., and R. Routledge (1990). "Estimating the Size of Criminal Populations." *Journal of Quantitative Criminology*, 6:293-314.

Vancouver Local Areas, 1971-1981 (1985). Vancouver: City of Vancouver Planning Department.

Chapter 10

Problem Solving and Crime Prevention in Public Housing*

Lucy Edwards Hochstein & Quint C. Thurman

Introduction

Tacoma, Washington, is a large, urbanized city with a substantial downtown and an inner-city residential area with numerous apartment complexes known as Hilltop. By the early 1990s Tacoma had become a suburb of its sprawling neighbor, Seattle, and Hilltop had evolved into a crime-ridden ghetto of absentee slum landlords, drug dealing, drive-by shootings, ethnic gang clashes, and extreme poverty. The growth of crime in Hilltop was moving criminal activities beyond Hilltop into previously safe Tacoma neighborhoods. Even though many Tacoma residents commute daily to the greater Seattle area, they spend their weekends and evenings in Tacoma, where their presence resulted in a proportionate increase in the opportunity for criminal victimization.

Background

Residents of more and more Tacoma neighborhoods were becoming victimized due to the spread of crime beyond Hilltop. State and national media coverage of Hilltop crimes and the spread of crime into previously safe neighborhoods were causing erosion of Tacoma's economic base. Businesses were leaving because their employees would not live in the unsafe city, and new businesses could not be attracted. Lower socioeconomic-level residents could not find safe, affordable housing. Increases in police calls for service were putting a large dent in the city's budget. Citizen activists and business leaders who did not abandon Tacoma were demanding substantial changes.

*This chapter is adapted from a chapter that originally appeared in *Contemporary Policing: Controversies, Challenges, and Solutions*, by Quint Thurman and Jihong Zhao (eds.), copyright © 2004 by Roxbury Pubishing. Reprinted by permission of Roxbury Publishing.

Problem-Solving Approach

Crime Free Multi-Family Housing (CFMFH) was initially introduced in Tacoma as a pilot project in 1996. CFMFH was a collaborative effort with the Tacoma Police Department, the Tacoma Fire Department, Tacoma Building and Land Use Services, and the Tacoma Human Rights Department that received a grant from the Washington Governor's Office of Juvenile Justice (a division of the Department of Social and Health Services). Designed to increase collaboration between local agencies, businesses, neighborhoods, and individuals to create a useful and replicable program that might be applied in any community under similar circumstances, CFMFH was developed to achieve objectives related to the education, inspection, and certification of the area's apartment communities. These objectives included reduction of calls for police services, especially those involving juvenile crime; increases in prosocial youth activities; provision of landlord information regarding eviction and intervention; facilitation of voluntary certification of rental units; and creation of city ordinances that promoted continuation of the project beyond its initial funding.

To achieve its objectives, CFMFH featured four main components. The *landlord component* required participating multifamily rental property managers and owners to attend a 16-hour training seminar on crime prevention practices and policies for reducing the opportunity for criminal activities that typically occur on their premises. A key strategy emphasized during the training, and required for certification as a CFMFH housing structure, was the development of standardized procedures to screen out undesirable tenant applicants. Each apartment manager or landlord was trained to use criminal background checks paid for by a $60 tenant application fee to regulate those applying to lease rental space. Only applicants without felony convictions were allowed occupancy, and application fees were not returned to rejected applicants, thus creating a disincentive for felons to continue to seek residence in other CFMFH complexes once they were turned down.

The second component provided participants with a *Crime Prevention Through Environmental Design (CPTED) evaluation* of their property and then allowed the opportunity to apply for CPTED certification. Sites that met the assessment criteria were expected to incur less risk for criminal activity than those that either failed to comply or did not apply for certification in the first place.

The third CFMFH component involved *tenant education*. Residents were offered information they could use to reduce their personal or familial vulnerability to criminal victimization. The fourth component was the *After-School Latchkey Program*. This program was designed to provide youth in the targeted area with activities that promote increased self-esteem, social skills, and continuity in the rapidly changing environment of low-income families.

Although the CFMFH program's target area encompasses the entire city of Tacoma, there was special emphasis on neighborhoods or housing complexes that had fallen victim to urban decay, such as Hilltop. Apartment complexes in these neighborhoods were all several decades old, and most were in need of extensive repair. These neighborhoods were generally characterized by a low-income, poorly educated, elderly, single-parent, or transient population and had at one time witnessed or experienced high incidences of drug and gang activity, prostitution, and other related crime and social disorder problems. Tenants were of all ages, ranging from children to the elderly, and represented various ethnic backgrounds.

While program personnel focused on these first-order program participants, they also expanded the scope of the program over time to include less seriously afflicted complexes. However, key program strategies continued to be education, inspection, and certification of apartment communities, with the corresponding objectives of police service call reduction, prosocial youth activities, intervention and eviction information for landlords, rental unit registration, and the creation of city ordinances in support of the program.

Results

Tacoma's CFMFH project was evaluated in 1998, 1999, and 2000. Data from those evaluations revealed that Tacoma apartment managers and owners, citizen activists, and government and business leaders credit CFMFH as a force for positive physical and social change. People familiar with Tacoma's multifamily apartment complexes credited CFMFH with many favorable outcomes, such as expanded rapport with police, a stronger sense of community, pride in apartments' appearances and premises, concern with elimination of undesirable people and activities, and increased awareness of the responsibilities involved in maintaining a positive equilibrium within the neighborhood.

Between 1998 and 2000, 30 percent of the city's multifamily rental properties became certified, and 411 managers and landlords participated in the training program. Not every trained manager and landlord had their building certified, but they often tightened their rental and screening policies, called police about illegal activities, and took action against problem tenants, as do managers and owners of certified properties.

Drug and gang problems in some areas of Tacoma became almost nonexistent over the first three years of the program. Overall police calls for service continued to drop during the same time period. Police calls for service to multifamily rental properties with CFMFH-trained owners or managers usually dramatically increase through the first quarter after training. During and after the second quarter of training, calls usually drop off significantly and stay reduced over time. Calls for police service did not decrease at every location. Increases in calls appear to be an indication of a growing concern for what is going on in the neighborhood rather than turning a blind eye to crime or feeling helpless to act in negative situations. Managers and tenants shared a new feeling of safety and security within the home environment.

Improvements made to apartment complexes throughout the city were both aesthetically and substantively significant. Managers, owners, business leaders, and civic activists now see Tacoma as a better place for citizens of all socioeconomic levels to live and as a much more economically attractive locale for new businesses to locate. Law-abiding, low-income citizens now have safe places to rent in a safe environment and have been empowered to participate in maintaining the safety of their neighborhoods.

A secondary effect of the project is that those applicants who have been determined ineligible for tenancy in CFMFH properties have been forced to move to outlying areas that have not yet adopted the program. While this may help to eliminate crime problems in Tacoma apartment complexes, it has largely displaced these problems to fringe areas of neighboring towns.

Factors that appear to have been most instrumental in bringing about positive CFMFH results appear to be twofold: commitment of project personnel and City of Tacoma departmental directors, and allegiance of managers and landlords. Their involvement and concern for the project's success serve as focal points for other participants. Project personnel work beyond normal working hours to encourage program participation.

Managers and landlords expressed genuine concern and personal investment in their properties and were outspoken as to the lengths to which they would go in order to maintain the standards they had recently come to enjoy. They encourage others in their neighborhoods to participate and work with them to make changes that improve the environment for all of their neighbors.

The city's departmental directors used all means at their disposal to support the program. For example, cooperation between the Tacoma Fire Department and the Human Rights Department allowed the fire department to force substandard apartment complexes to be vacated and found alternative housing for residents, putting pressure on slum landlords to make their buildings safe or risk complete loss of income. The Tacoma Police Department and the Human Rights Department trained landlords and managers in the state of Washington's landlord-tenant act as well as in identification of criminal behavior such as domestic violence and drug production and dealing. Under the landlord-tenant act perpetrators can be evicted without notice. Tacoma Building and Land Use Services had ordinances passed that prevented building windows from being boarded up for more than two weeks. Keeping windows repaired in derelict buildings encouraged many owners to tear down these buildings, which provided building lots for new construction in the inner city. Absentee landlords are now required to provide contact information for their agents, who must live within 10 miles of the owners' properties.

When grant funding expires, programs often have a difficult time finding local funding, and important program components are lost. At the end of the three-year grant period, the director of the Public Works Department—a strong supporter of the CFMFH project—committed to funding one-third of the current program and challenged other city departments to match his funding. This support reflects the many visible changes in Tacoma due to the CFMFH program.

Conclusion

Project personnel provide official support for the efforts being made in Tacoma's multifamily housing community complexes to improve themselves, and also serve as the link between citizens and their municipal administration.

Stakeholder interviews and observations of participating properties revealed that improvements were not only significant aesthetically but were also enduring. Thus the program appears to offer more than a "band-aid" approach to a serious problem, and provides much more than temporary relief.

References

Brantingham, P.J., and P.L. Brantingham (1981). *Environmental Criminology.* Beverly Hills, CA: Sage Publications.

Burgess, E.W. (1916). "Juvenile Delinquency in a Small City." *Journal of the American Institute of Criminal Law and Criminology* 6:724-728.

Lurigio, A.J., and D.P. Rosenbaum (1986). "Evaluation Research in Community Crime Prevention: A Critical Look at the Field." In D.P. Rosenbaum (ed.), *Community Crime Prevention: Does It Work?* Beverly Hills, CA: Sage Publications.

McGarrell, E.F., A.L. Giacomazzi, Q.C. Thurman, and R. Lincoln (1996). "Reducing Fear and Crime in Public Housing: Effects of a Drug Crime Elimination Program in Spokane, WA." Spokane: Washington State University.

Rosenbaum, D.P. (1986). "The Problem of Crime Control." In D.P. Rosenbaum (ed.), *Community Crime Prevention: Does it Work?* Beverly Hills, CA: Sage Publications.

Shaw, C.R., and H.D. McKay (1931). "Social Factors in Juvenile Delinquency." *Report on the Causes of Crime*, vol. 2. Washington, DC: U.S. Government Printing Office.

Wilson, J.Q., and G. Kelling (1982). "Broken Windows." *The Atlantic Monthly* 249:29-38.

Section IV

Advanced Problem Solving and Problem-Specific Strategies

Chapter 11

Foretelling Crimes of the Future Using Crimes of the Past: Analyzing Repeat Victimization

Kenneth J. Peak & Ronald W. Glensor

Introduction

The premise underlying repeat victimization is that if you want to know where a crime will occur *next,* look at where it happened *last.* This premise may be considered to be at the heart of crime prevention. Crime prevention, furthermore, is at the heart of problem-oriented policing; the best solution to crime problems is to prevent them from occurring. This approach places offenders in a larger context, it shifts the focus from looking at why people commit crime to looking primarily at why crime occurs with specific persons and in specific settings. The emphasis is on trying to reduce the opportunities for crime.

This chapter examines the concept of repeat victimization in terms of its extent and rationale. It is argued that an understanding of this concept is essential to better identify complex crime patterns and predict criminal activity. Also emphasized is the relationship between repeat victimization and the problem-solving process.

Background

Repeat victimization is a relatively new approach to crime analysis and prevention. Repeat victimization occurs when the same person or place suffers from more than one incident over a specified period (Bridgeman & Hobbs, 1997) and is arguably the best single predictor routinely available to the police in the absence of specific intelligence information. Just as a small percentage of offenders accounts for a disproportionate amount of crime, so does a small percentage of victims account for a disproportionate number of victimizations. And just as high-rate offenders typically commit many different types of crime, high-rate victims fall prey to a variety of victimizations (Farrell, 1995).

Most research on repeat victimization has been conducted in Great Britain. For example, it has been determined that five percent of respondents who experienced five or more victimizations suffered 43 percent of all crimes reported; in addition, half of those victimized were repeat victims and suffered 81 percent of reported crimes. Another research summary (National Board for Crime Prevention, 1994) found the following:

- Only 10 percent of domestic violence represented an isolated event.

- Once burglarized, a residence is reburglarized at four times the rate of unburglarized homes.

- More than 39 percent of small businesses were found to have been reburglarized at least once a year.

Additionally, Anderson et al. (1995) found that revictimization within 11 months for nonresidential burglary was 28 percent, and for residential burglary, 16 percent. In fact, research in Britain concerning burglaries has determined that in some 80 percent of cases where more than one burglary is cleared with an arrest, the perpetrator is the same person.

Repeat victimization research in the United States suggests that one in three burglaries is a repeat burglary of a household already burglarized. Elsewhere in the world, one study of 11 other countries found that the proportion of repeat burglaries is higher in the United States than in Finland, the Netherlands, Switzerland, France, Northern Ireland, Canada, Sweden, England and Wales, Austria, and Sweden. This means that at least one-third of all burglaries in the United States might be avoided if repeated burglaries were prevented. Furthermore, a large proportion of other crimes happen to the same victims, including 48 percent of the repeated victimizations found for sexual incidents (including grabbing, touching, and assault), 43 percent for assaults and threats, and 23 percent for vehicle vandalism (Farrell & Sousa, 1997). In addition, a domestic study of white-collar crime (Alexander, personal communication to Farrell & Sousa, 1997) indicated that the same people are victims of fraud and embezzlement over and over, and that banks also have high rates of repeat robbery victimization (Pease, personal communication to Farrell & Sousa, 1997).

What are some rationales for repeat victimization occurring? Consider burglary as an example. Why do burglars return to burglarize the same household? It could be argued that it makes sense to return because temporary repairs to a burglarized home will make a subsequent burglary easier, the burglar has become familiar with the physical layout and surroundings of the property, the burglar knows what items of value were left behind at the prior burglary, and the burglar also knows that items taken at the previous burglary are likely to have been replaced through insurance.

Research has determined that people also experience repeat victimization for reasons primarily relating to their place of residence, chaotic lifestyles, and bad relationships. It also is known that repeat victimization is:

- *Predictable*—once victimized, a person or place is more likely to be victimized again than one that has not.

- *Rapid*—second and subsequent offenses follow fairly rapidly after the first.

- *Highest in high-crime areas*—certain areas have high crime rates not because more people are victimized, but because there is more victimization of the same people.

Simply stated, victims are targeted repeatedly by criminals for two basic reasons: (1) risk assessment by offenders (for example, a secluded house with poor lighting and no security will be regarded as low-risk by the passing burglar); and (2) victimization itself makes a repeat more likely. In sum, the following assertions can be made with reasonable confidence concerning repeat victimizations (Farrell, 1995):

- An individual's past crime victimization is a good predictor of his or her subsequent victimization.

- The greater the number of prior victimizations, the higher the likelihood the victim will experience future crime (Pease & Laycock, 1996).

- Especially within crime-prone areas, a substantial percentage of victimizations consists of repeat victims (Pease & Laycock, 1996).

- If victimization recurs, it tends to do so soon after the prior occurrence, especially for residential burglary, domestic violence, auto crimes, and retail crimes (Farrell & Pease, 1993). In residential burglary, 40 percent of repeat burglaries occur within one month of the previous burglary (Anderson et al., 1995). This can be a result of event dependence or risk heterogeneity. Under event dependence, a first crime will itself make later crimes more likely or linked through a prior event. Thus, a burglar's inability to carry all of the valuable items from the burglarized home may make a return visit likely. Furthermore, temporary repairs to this burglarized home will make subsequent burglaries easier. Under risk heterogeneity, places and people at high risk, and in consequence suffering many crimes, will thus suffer frequent crimes (Pease, 1996:4).

- The same perpetrators seem to be responsible for the bulk of repeated offenses against a victim (Pease & Laycock, 1996).

- Many factors, from police shift patterns to computer systems, conspire to mask the true contribution of repeat victimization to the general crime problem (Pease & Laycock, 1996).

Problem-Solving Approach

The root of the four-stage problem-solving method known as SARA (Eck & Spelman, 1987:43-52) lies in the structured analysis of problems. The process leads law enforcement officers to look for clusters of similar, related, or recurring incidents rather than a single incident.

Although problem-oriented policing and repeat victimization may be viewed as separate and distinct concepts, both involve a structured analysis of crime problems, and both approaches are engaged before an incident occurs. They prompt law enforcement officers to move beyond just handling incidents to recognizing that incidents are merely overt symptoms of problems, and to understand the relationships between incidents.

The means and the need exist for identifying the "hot spots" (places) and "hot dots" (a new term for victims who repeatedly suffer crime). Key sources for obtaining repeat victimization information are:

> **Police records:** the police use data from their crime-recording system or incident logs.
>
> **Other agencies' records:** for example, in examining school crime, school records may provide a more complete picture.
>
> **Crime victims:** information may be gleaned from victims concerning how (method of operation), when, and what happened (Bridgeman & Hobbs, 1997:6).

After collecting the information, the police then analyze it, preferably over a 12-month period, seeking patterns within and among the following types of analyses:

> *Location-driven analysis:* focuses on the geographical location of the incident or offense.

Object-driven analysis: similar to location, but is used when the location is not fixed. An example would be an investigation of crimes against motor vehicles that concentrates on the individual vehicle rather than the location.

Victim-driven analysis: some forms of repeat victimization, such as racially motivated crimes, will focus on the victim.

Hot spot-driven analysis: refers to a site that accounts for a disproportionate number of crimes or incidents. It may refer to a single location (such as a house or a park), or a wider area (such as a particular street or neighbourhood). The ultimate hot spot, the "hot dot," is the individual victim who repeatedly suffers crime (Bridgeman & Hobbs, 1997:7-8).

Once this analysis has been completed, police officers can make an informed decision about where to concentrate their problem-solving efforts. This analysis helps to identify repeat offenders, problem locations (hot spots), and victims, and then to develop appropriate, tailor-made responses to the problems.

Results

The following case study demonstrates how the police can take affirmative measures to address repeat victimization. Crime analyses in London indicated that 74 of 172 (43%) of domestic violence incidents occurring over a 25-month period involved only about seven percent of 1,450 households (Lloyd et al., 1994). Police took the following measures to help prevent recurrence, to apprehend batterers, and to enhance the victims' sense of security:

1. *Development and distribution of neck-pendant alarms to repeat victims.* When a person presses the button on the pendant, it dials a central station that triggers a priority response from police, opens a voice channel so the police can hear what is happening, and provides assurance that help is on the way.

2. *Improvement in the transfer of injunction information from courts to police.* Police knowledge of injunctions against batterers permits officers to arrive on the scene with a better understanding of their legal authority with the incident at hand.

3. *Provision of support and information for victims.* Police employed a domestic violence specialist who developed safety plans for victims and helped them to improve their communication with other agencies (Pease & Laycock, 1996).

These measures were warmly received by the police and victims alike, and several arrests were made as a result.

Conclusion

Repeat victimization is not new; police officers have always been aware that the same people and places are victimized again and again. However, what is new are attempts abroad to incorporate repeat victimization knowledge into formal crime prevention efforts. Research has enabled the police to bring repeat victimization into clearer focus and has indicated what must be done—and the kinds of information systems required—to identify locations and people who need the kind of crime prevention attention that is offered through this concept.

British police forces seek to implement repeat victimization policy as daily practice. Police in the United States would do well to also recognize the value of including repeat victimization in their overall crime management policy.

References

Anderson, D., S. Chenery, and K. Pease (1994). "Biting Back: Tackling Repeat Burglary and Car Crime." *Crime Detection and Prevention Papers* 58. London: Home Office Police Research Group Briefing Note.

Anderson, D., S. Chenery, and K. Pease (1995). "Preventing Repeat Victimization: A Report on Progress in Huddersfield." London: Home Office Police Research Group Briefing Note 4/95.

Bridgeman, C., and L. Hobbs (1997). "Preventing Repeat Victimisation: The Police Officer's Guide." London: Home Office Police Research Group.

Eck, J.E., and W. Spelman (1987). "Problem-Oriented Policing." Washington, DC: National Institute of Justice.

Farrell, G. (1995). "Preventing Repeat Victimization." In M. Tonry and D.P. Farrington (eds.), *Building a Safer Society: Strategic Approaches to Crime Prevention*. Chicago: University of Chicago Press.

Farrell, G., and K. Pease (1993). "Once Bitten, Twice Bitten: Repeat Victimization and Its Implications for Crime Prevention." Paper 46:3. London: Home Office Police Research Group, Crime Prevention Unit.

Farrell, G., and W. Sousa (1997). "Repeat Victimization in the United States and Ten Other Industrialized Countries." Paper presented at the National Conference on Preventing Crime, Washington, D.C., October 13.

Lloyd, S., G. Farrell, and K. Pease (1994). "Preventing Repeated Domestic Violence: A Demonstration Project on Merseyside." London: Home Office Police Research Group, Crime Prevention Unit Paper 49.

Pease, K. (1996). "Repeat Victimization and Policing." Unpublished manuscript, University of Huddersfield, West Yorkshire, England, June 30:4.

Pease, K., and G. Laycock (1996). "Revictimization: Reducing the Heat on Hot Victims." *NIJ Research in Action*. Washington, DC: National Institute of Justice.

Chapter 12

Problem Solving Investigations*

Brian Forst

Introduction

Although the central role of criminal investigators is to solve crimes that have occurred in the past, many current and future day-to-day problems confronting criminal investigators can be alleviated through more conscious investments in identifying and solving problems that are manifested in *patterns*. Problem-oriented policing has changed much regarding how police think about and do their work toward this end, but it has been applied primarily as a strategy for patrol operations. Some criminal investigation problems that lend themselves to this strategy are unique to particular settings, and some are common to criminal investigation generally. Specific areas of opportunity for substantial improvement in problem-oriented investigation include collaboration with patrol officers, shift of focus from offenses to offenders and locations, and a more coherent use of modus operandi files and related data sources. This chapter explores the application of problem identification and problem-solving tools to these and other issues in criminal investigation.

*This chapter is adapted from one that appeared first in *Readings in Problem-Oriented Policing*, edited by Tara O'Connor Shelley and Anne C. Grant (Washington, DC: Police Executive Research Forum, 1998). The author wishes to thank Adam Lankford for thoughtful help in revising the material, and John Eck, Michael Planty, and Ross Swope for their helpful comments on the earlier work. Reproduced with permission from the Police Executive Research Forum.

Background

The application of preventive, problem-oriented approaches to criminal investigation is inherently limited. Criminal investigation is, after all, primarily about solving crimes that have already occurred. The investigator becomes involved typically after preventive policing strategies have already failed. Moreover, the investigator responds to a single incident that may or may not be related to other incidents, while "problems" in problem-oriented policing are clusters of related incidents, not single incidents (Goldstein, 1990:66).

Nonetheless, the stages noted above—problem identification, data collection, and problem solving—apply to most investigations as well. An unsolved crime *is* a problem—its solution, prior research has found, depends more on whether the victims and witnesses identify the offenders than it does on keen powers of detective reasoning and intuition or cutting-edge forensic analysis (Greenwood et al., 1975). By investing in building closer ties with the community, the police can encourage critical sources of information to come forth when they are needed to help in solving particular crimes. Problem-solving processes are called for, moreover, to reveal patterns of crime so that future crimes that follow such patterns can be prevented.

In the natural course of conducting a long series of investigations, detectives become aware of patterns that may provide opportunities for crime prevention. Such patterns can often be more quickly and sharply identified through crime analysis, the process of identifying and describing trends and patterns in the commission of crimes based on analysis of data (Taylor, 2002; Eck & Weisburd, 1995; Reuland, 1997; Reinier et al., 1977). Of particular interest in crime analysis are the following questions: *Where* have particular kinds of crimes been occurring? *When* have they been occurring—at particular times of day, day of week or month, season of the year, or under particular sets of circumstances? What specific *similarities* and *dissimilarities* exist among crimes that have been occurring at crime "hot spots"? Which of the similarities suggests a particular offender or group of offenders? What do similarities among or patterns about the victims suggest? For example, is the same type of vehicle being broken into? Are elderly people being targeted? Who might have additional information regarding these patterns—information that could solve the crime or lead to a solution? While the patterns unearthed by addressing such questions may occasionally be distinct enough to permit predictions of specific crime occurrences, they are more likely only to suggest areas that should be closely monitored at certain times.

John Eck has described instances of detectives taking such a view of investigative work. One example is that of a detective in Newport News, Virginia, who speculated that half of the homicides in that city (those following domestic disputes) may be preventable through more effective early intervention strategies. By bringing together local experts in the field of domestic violence to review current procedures and explore opportunities for more effective intervention, the detective helped to develop a new program that forced targeted couples into mandatory counseling (Eck, 1996).

Specific data sources can be especially useful in crime analysis. Crime reports give basic information about the category of crime, time and place of occurrence, and the victim. Dispatch records provide basic data about the response to each reported incident to which a unit or units were sent. Activity summaries supply information about what was observed at the scene, names of witnesses and suspicious persons, and dispositions of each matter. Modus operandi files were used to help solve new crimes and furnish information about commonalities among crimes, both those committed by specific offenders known to the department and those committed by unidentified offenders. These data sources typically vary in degrees of computer readability and reliability, depending on the department.

Some jurisdictions have developed their own unique data systems useful for supporting crime analysis. The state of Washington created a system in 1990 to assist in solving homicides: the Homicide Investigation and Tracking System (HITS). Allowing for as many as 250 data elements in a single record, the system documents information about victims, crime scene details, and people arrested for the crime (Keppel & Weis, 1993).

Because a problem-oriented approach is more generalized than the by-the-book approach common in policing, it has implications for a different set of management conventions. It calls first for a more decentralized decision-making authority. Investigators and patrol officers cannot be expected to find creative solutions to problems when they must obtain approval from a supervisor at each and every decision point. For major decisions, approval will be needed, which suggests a second requirement: a problem-oriented strategy requires training and policy guidance of mid-managers so that they can respond effectively to questions from less senior personnel.

Perhaps most important, a problem-oriented approach inolves risks. It requires that management be willing to experience occasional failures—especially personnel time spent on activities that yield no apparent results—to prevent future crimes. When an officer's, detective's, or unit's occasional failures outweigh the value associated with problems identified and solved over a period of months, it becomes appropriate to review the specific problem-solving objectives and procedures employed by the individual or unit. Such a review may turn up any of several possible flaws: inadequate training in problem solving, objectives that do not appear to contribute immediately to the performance measures used to assess the unit, insufficient use of available information sources, or simply a lack of commitment to the approach, sometimes to the extent that "problem solving" is used as a ruse for malingering.

When problem-solving or crime analysis unearths problems or patterns that may be endemic to the larger community, it is important that the insights be disseminated (by way of internal memoranda, bulletins, "hot sheets," or maps) to other individuals and units that may be able to use the

information. Resources may be reallocated, decoys and stings may be established, targets may be hardened, and decisions and policies may be recon-
sidered in light of such information.

Specific areas of opportunity for substantial improvement in problem-
oriented investigation include collaboration with patrol officers and others,
shifts of focus from offenses to offenders and locations, improvements in
criminal profiling, and a more coherent usage of modus operandi files and
related data sources. Each of these areas is addressed below.

Problem-Solving Approach

Several characteristics of traditional investigative methods may be
improved with problem-solving orientation. These characteristics are:

1. Limited coordination between detectives generally;

2. A tendency to focus on individual offenses;

3. The limited use and scope of profiling resources;

4. The limited use of modus operandi files.

Detectives almost never solve crimes without help from others. They typically receive a case from the patrol officer who conducted a preliminary
investigation at the crime scene. They often work with officers from other
jurisdictions to exchange information about suspects in a case or series of
cases. They work closely with patrol officers assigned to the beats in which
the crime occurred to obtain information from other informed sources in the
area—information that often turns out to be the difference between a solved
and an unsolved crime.

Coordination has become critically important in most contemporary settings.
Communities have turned increasingly to private solutions to crime prevention, and for serious commercial and residential crimes police investigators must work effectively with private security agents to obtain information
leading to solved crimes and to the prevention of future crimes. Community
policing strategies also call for increased coordination with public and private institutions (social service agencies, churches, public utilities, and so
on) to solve crimes, aid victims, and prevent future crimes. Patrol officers
often perform many of these coordinating activities, but investigators cannot always leave these matters for patrol officers to do alone.

Coordination begins with effective communication. Communication is
sometimes formal, sometimes informal. Formal communication is preferable in a variety of circumstances: when important information needs to be
given precisely and systematically, when the information needs to be pre-
served (for example, to be used later in court), or when sensitive informa-

tion cannot be effectively presented in person—for example, because it may be easily distorted or misunderstood. Informal communication is more appropriate when flexibility is needed, when real meanings must be conveyed that are not clear in formal modes, when formal modes are too costly, or when a personal touch is needed to stimulate unity. Informal communication has expanded considerably in the information and communication technology boom of the era, and further gains are likely as investigators continue to purposefully add Internet, e-mail resources, and media to their more traditional array of tools.

Effective communication serves a multitude of purposes. It informs and educates, providing essential information clearly. It serves to unite, often by resolving controversy and facilitating the redress of grievances. It motivates by showing respect and assurance, avoiding threats, soliciting ideas, giving reasons behind directives and basic information, and by listening as well as transmitting information. It can improve operations by stimulating useful feedback information and cooperation.

In short, detectives can more accurately identify problems, obtain better information about them, and develop more effective solution strategies by improving their coordination with others who have information and insights about the problems.

A shift in focus from offenses to offenders and locations of crime would improve general investigative effectiveness. Case-oriented investigation is the traditional reactive method of handling an unsolved crime. Usually the result of a patrol officer's response to a call for service, the investigation's magnitude is determined primarily by the gravity of the offense rather than the dangerousness of the suspect or the relationship between the current crime and other matters of concern in the area. Serious crimes generally lend themselves to case-oriented investigation.

Case-oriented investigations do not ignore offender information or information about problems in the area that may be related. Information about offenders and related problems can help lead to the crime's solution and the offender's arrest. These matters, however, are not the primary information goals of case-oriented investigation. They are subordinated to the primary goal of case-oriented investigation, which is to obtain information to solve a single crime. Thus, the focus of case-oriented investigation is on the physical evidence, information provided by victims and witnesses about suspects, information about a suspect's vehicle, the recovery of stolen property, and modus operandi information that can lead to a solution of the crime.

Case-oriented investigations are often required even in environments that make full use of preventive strategies. Such investigations can, in any case, employ modern methods of crime solving, including the use of solvability factors to focus resources on the most effective aspects of the case (Greenwood et al., 1975).

Offender-oriented investigations focus on people who are known to have committed specific crimes and may be suspected of having committed several others in the area. This tactic is more proactive than the case-oriented strategy; it anticipates and heads off new crimes by focusing resources on people who have already established themselves as offenders. The basic concept of an offender-oriented approach derives from a widely observed finding that a few offenders are responsible for a disproportionate number of crimes and that investigative resources can be more productively applied to cases involving those offenders than to cases involving the less frequent and less dangerous offender.

Investigators have long appreciated the value of offender-oriented investigation. The Federal Bureau of Investigation, following Henry Fielding's published descriptions of wanted persons in *The Covent Garden Journal* and Allan Pinkerton's publication of a "rogues' gallery" of offenders, first created its list of "Ten Most Wanted" in the United States in the 1930s. Several local police departments followed suit. Even prosecutors set up programs focusing on repeat offenders and major violators in the 1970s. While some of those lists and programs targeted offenders who had been put there primarily because of the nature of a single crime rather than a series of crimes, the strategies were nonetheless offender-based rather than offense-based.

National databases such as that maintained by the National Crime Information Center (NCIC) can be especially helpful in supporting offender-based investigation strategies. The Violent Criminal Apprehension Program (VICAP) is a national program run by the FBI to link homicide cases committed by the same offender (Green & Whitmore, 1993). Systems such as California's CAL-ID and the Automated Wants and Warrants System (AWWS) and Michigan's Law Enforcement Information Network (LEIN) provide somewhat comparable offender-based information at the state level. Effective offender-based systems are typically automated, with fingerprint data, criminal history records, and information about crime locations, stolen property, license registration, and DNA patterns of convicted sex offenders (Reaves, 1995).

Improved profiling procedures also would improve general investigative effectiveness. Profiling has become an established procedure of criminal investigation, and it can be a powerful tool in solving problems and reducing future crimes. The central purpose of profiling is to prevent crimes through targeting likely sources and settings, but profiling may also free up resources to solve crimes previously committed more quickly and effectively. Profiling aims to organize scarce law enforcement resources in a way that is logical and focused rather than random or arbitrary, in both its police-initiated preventive and reactive crime-solving applications. Profiling is widely used in areas in which the police have a variety of options for resource allocation and moderate to high levels of crime.

The decision to initiate a police interrogation or search in the absence of a call for service may be based on time and place, on situation, on the characteristics of frequently offending individuals, or, more typically, on various combinations of the three.

When based on *time and place*, perhaps the product of "hot spot" policing (Sherman, 2002) or geographic profiling (see Chapter 13), crime might be more effectively controlled, but possibly at the expense of imposing inconvenience costs on innocent people in the area at the time. Arrests that follow this sort of targeting are useful when they reduce crime, provided that the inconvenience costs to others are not excessive.

When based on *situation*—for example, people behaving suspiciously just outside of a bar occasioned by frequent assault, or in a parking lot that is the scene of a rash of thefts—the conditions observed must satisfy the legal standard of "reasonable suspicion" in order for the police to have legal justification for a search without a court-issued warrant. The reasonable suspicion standard is less stringent than that of "probable cause" needed for the police to make an arrest or search an automobile without a warrant. In jurisdictions or cases involving officers who are inexperienced or inadequately screened and trained and thus unprepared to conduct situational profiling with the prudent exercise of discretion, mandatory arrest policies may be preferable.

Profiling based on characteristics of suspects is often essential, but is also the most controversial, as most of the people who have the characteristics under suspicion are likely to be innocent and lacking any intent to commit a future crime. Proponents see this sort of profiling as critical for enabling investigators to solve serious crimes by restricting the suspect pool to manageable proportions and identifying offenders more quickly, often through the use of a variety of forensic practices (Holmes, 1998; Turvey, 2002). The profile information can also be used subsequently to guide the suspect interrogation and other aspects of the investigation (Miethe & McCorkle, 2001).

When based purely on intuition or unconfirmed speculation, without empirical validation, profiling can be ineffective at best and divisively harmful to the community at worst (Forst, 2004; Canter, 2000; Muller, 2000). To civil libertarians, profiling is especially toxic when police action is based on ethnicity rather than behavior, when it results in the arrest and harassment of disproportionate numbers of persons from disadvantaged minority groups, a practice that has come to be known as "racial profiling" (Kennedy, 1997). Using ethnicity as a factor in profiling is unjustifiable when its relationship to a crime is unfounded or when it is used in place of factors that are related to a crime. It is especially unjustifiable when used as a ruse, as when a trivial traffic violation is arbitrarily applied as a lever to allow the police to search the member of a minority group for weapons or drugs.

In the extreme, profiling is either an effective crime-solving approach or a sure-fire way to multiply due process errors, institutionalize racism, and reduce police legitimacy, further limiting the ability of the police to obtain

POLICE PROBLEM SOLVING

support from the community in solving crimes. As is the case with most criminal justice practices, the truth is more complicated. Confusion about profiling has been exacerbated by the fact that the term "profiling" has several different meanings, depending on whether it is used to prevent crimes or apprehend a particular offender; to develop a psychological picture of a particular offender, usually an intuitive process; or to fit a particular pattern of offending with a more general criminal archetype, which is more conducive to empirical methods.

A more coherent use of modus operandi files and related data sources would increase the general level of investigative effectiveness. Well-designed and carefully maintained modus operandi (MO) files often prove useful as well. Modus operandi files provide information about the method of operation of suspects associated with particular cases: method of entry, tools and weapons used, victim characteristics and behaviors, crime scene condition, and so on.

Although the use of MO files appears to vary substantially from department to department, they can be used to identify offenders in new cases, sometimes by linking characteristics of the new cases to patterns that show up in prior solved cases. The files can also be used to link new cases to patterns that show up in prior unsolved cases, providing opportunities to combine information from different crimes to build a stronger basis for solving a series of crimes committed by a single offender. Such links can be used to set up surveillance and undercover operations to catch the offender in a subsequent crime, or to prevent further crimes by increasing security for victims or targets that fit the prior patterns.

Conclusion

Problem-oriented strategies can be used to improve contemporary criminal investigation in several ways. One is to expand effective collaborations both within police departments, by investigators working more effectively with patrol officers, and also with investigators and officers in other law enforcement agencies. This involves not only more effective personal outreach to break down artificial territorial boundaries within and between departments, but improvements in data-sharing technologies and activities as well. Offenders who commit crimes in several different jurisdictions pose substantial problems across the map. They often evade capture due to failures of different jurisdictions to coordinate with one another and to share data. Problems confronted by investigators in several places can be solved simultaneously by improving the flow of information from department to department across jurisdictional boundaries.

Another way to expand problem-oriented investigation opportunities is to improve the quality of information contained in existing data systems, including MO files. Modus operandi files could be improved through standardized data and organization of information and systematic procedures for correcting and updating the data. Recent estimates suggest that the likelihood that an offender in a new case had been arrested previously (and thus should be in the MO file) is considerably higher than is widely understood, and it rises substantially with increases in the probability of arrest and the average number of offenses in a criminal career (Forst & Planty, 2000). Improving MO files could have a multiplier effect: better MO files could induce increases in solution rates, increasing the probability of arrest, which could in turn induce victims to report crimes at a higher rate, thus providing still greater increases in the likelihood that the offender in a new case will be apprehended.

Criminal investigators are generally less visible to the public than are patrol officers. Their lower-profile status may allow them to focus more on solving crimes, but it may also tend to produce insularity, reducing incentives to build closer relationships with the community, as has become more common in patrol operations employing community- and problem-oriented policing strategies. Aspects of crime solving may be inherently more reactive than preventive, but problem-oriented policing is only superficially more relevant to patrol operations than to detective work. Investigators and patrol officers alike are bound to improve their performance by combining a focus on offenses with a focus on offenders and locations.

By combining traditional crime-solving methods with conscious investments in the identification and solution of *patterns* of problems that lie beneath the surface of one apparently unrelated case-oriented investigation after another, the thoughtful investigator and effective investigative unit can improve their ability to not only solve crimes but prevent them as well.

References

Canter, D. (2000). "Offender Profiling and Criminal Differentiation." *Journal of Legal and Criminological Psychology* 5:23-46.

Eck, J.E., and D. Weisburd (1995). "Crime Places in Crime Theory." In J.E. Eck and D. Weisburd (eds.), *Crime and Place,* Crime Prevention Studies, Vol. 4. Monsey, NY: Criminal Justice Press.

Eck, J.E. (1996). "Rethinking Detective Management." In L.T. Hoover (ed.), *Quantifying Quality in Policing*. Washington, DC: Police Executive Research Forum.

Forst, B. (2004). *Errors of Justice: Nature, Sources and Remedies*. New York: Cambridge University Press.

Forst, B., and M. Planty (2000). "What Is the Probability That the Offender in a New Case Is in the Modus Operandi File?" *International Journal of Police Science and Management* 3 (Winter 2000):124-37.

Goldstein, H. (1990). *Problem-Oriented Policing*. New York: McGraw-Hill.

Green, T., and J. Whitmore (1993). "VICAP's Role in Multiagency Serial Murder Investigations." *The Police Chief* 38-45.

Greenwood, P., J.M. Chaiken, J. Petersilia, and L. Prusoff (1975). *The Criminal Investigation Process.* Santa Monica, CA: RAND Corporation.

Holmes, R.M. (1998). "Psychological Profiling Use in Serial Murder Cases." In R.M. Holmes and S.T. Holmes (eds.), *Contemporary Perspectives on Serial Murder.* Thousand Oaks, CA: Sage Publications.

Kennedy, R. (1997). *Race, Crime, and the Law.* New York: Pantheon.

Keppel, R.D., and J.G. Weis (1993). "Improving the Investigation of Violent Crime: The Homicide Investigation and Tracking System." *National Institute of Justice Research in Brief.* Washington, DC: U.S. Department of Justice.

Miethe, T., and R. McCorkle (2001). *Crime Profiles: The Anatomy of Dangerous Persons, Places, and Situations.* Los Angeles: Roxbury.

Muller, D.A. (2000). "Criminal Profiling: Real Science or Just Wishful Thinking?" *Homicide Studies* 4:234-264.

Reaves, B.A. (1995). *Law Enforcement Management and Administrative Statistics.* Washington, DC: U.S. Department of Justice, Bureau of Justice Statistics.

Reinier, G.H., T.J. Sweeney, R.V. Waymire, R.A. Newton III, R.G. Grassie, S.M. White, and W.D. Wallace (1977). *Crime Analysis Operations Manual: Integrated Criminal Apprehension Program.* Washington, DC: Law Enforcement Assistance Administration.

Reuland, M.M. (ed.) (1997). *Information Management and Crime Analysis: Practitioners' Recipes for Success.* Washington, DC: Police Executive Research Forum.

Sherman, L.W. (2002). "Fair and Effective Policing." In J.Q. Wilson and J. Petersilia (eds.), *Crime: Public Policies for Crime Control.* Oakland, CA: ICS Press.

Taylor, R.B. (2002). "Physical Environment, Crime, Fear, and Resident-Based Control." In J.Q. Wilson and J. Petersilia (eds.), *Crime: Public Policies for Crime Control.* Oakland, CA: ICS Press.

Turvey, B.E. (2002). *Criminal Profiling: An Introduction to Behavioral Evidence Analysis,* Second Edition. San Diego, CA: Academic Press.

Chapter 13

Geographic Profiling as Problem Solving for Serial Crime

D. Kim Rossmo

Introduction

It is a familiar scene—the television detective sits at his paper-strewn desk, tie askew and head in hands, bemoaning the fact that he has no suspects in his murder case. In reality, however, the investigation of most "whodunit" crimes involves the exact opposite problem—too *many* suspects. This is somewhat unexpected but follows from the nature of the investigative process. The majority of homicide victims are killed by someone they have a relationship with. So the police detective typically works outward from the victim, looking at family members, friends, business associates, neighbors, and so forth.

But stranger and serial crime involve no such connection. The detective consequently has to consider groups of individuals: every sex offender in the state registry, everyone living in the immediate area, every owner of a blue van, every call phoned in to the tip line. These large categories of low-quality suspects create the problem of information overload; too many tips, too many suspects—but too few police resources.

Some examples illustrate the point. In a series of sexual assaults during 1998 in suburban Toronto, including a rape from which DNA evidence was obtained, the police developed 312 suspects. Budget considerations limited the number of feasible laboratory tests. Project Green Ribbon in Ontario, investigating the sex murders of two teenage girls from 1991 to 1992, collected 31,000 tips and 3,200 suspects in just nine months—including the killer, who was just a needle in this haystack. In the Green River Killer

121

case, 18,000 suspect names were entered in their database—so many that it took years for police to thoroughly follow up. Yet even this amazing number pales in comparison to the 268,000 names amassed during the Yorkshire Ripper investigation. It naturally follows that dealing with a high volume of suspects requires thousands of hours of police time, with a price tag to match.

Investigative information in complex stranger and serial crime cases must be intelligently and efficiently managed, and large numbers of suspects need to be prioritized. One advantage to investigators inherent in serial crime is the fact that there are more pieces to the puzzle, presenting an opportunity to detect underlying patterns. Geographic profiling takes advantage of this by analyzing the spatial patterns of serial crimes in order to determine where the offender most likely resides. It therefore provides one method of suspect prioritization.

Background

Stranger and Serial Crime

Most serial crime—whether murder, rape, robbery, or auto theft—is stranger crime. This is not surprising. If an offender is known to the victim of a reported crime, the former is usually apprehended, derailing any crime series at the start. But if the offender is unknown, then police arrest is not certain; under these circumstances it is possible for a crime series to develop. And while most criminal offenders are not serial, much crime is. Studies show that a small number of offenders are responsible for a disproportionate amount of crime. For example, in one study on paraphiliacs, researchers found that five percent of sex offenders committed 70 percent of the offenses (Abel, Mittelman & Becker, 1985).

Criminal Investigative Process

The process of criminal investigation involves two semi-independent objectives: (1) find the offender; and (2) prove his or her guilt. These do not have to happen in order; the police can be in the position of having achieved one of the objectives, both, or neither. If neither objective has been met, the crime is far from being solved; if both, then the case can proceed to trial. There are two possibilities if only one of the two objectives has been realized. When a woman is found murdered and police believe the husband is responsible but they lack sufficient evidence to charge him, the first, but not the second objective has been achieved. In the opinion of many, this is what has happened in the JonBenet Ramsey homicide in Boulder, Colorado, in 1996. Alternatively, when police have DNA or fingerprint evidence from a stranger crime scene but do not know who to compare it to, the second, but not the first objective has been achieved. This was the situation during the investigations of the Washington, D.C., sniper shootings and the Baton Rouge, Louisiana, serial murders. Ballistic evidence had been recovered in the former case, but investigators had not found the rifle they were looking for. DNA evidence was recovered in the latter case, but detectives did not initially know who to match it to.

There are only three possible ways to prove an individual's guilt: (1) witness; (2) confession; or (3) physical evidence (Klockars & Mastrofski, 1991). The first two are usually regarded as direct evidence, and the last as indirect or circumstantial evidence. But to find the perpetrator of a serial or stranger crime is a less straightforward process because of the problem of information overload. Finding offenders in such cases involves three separate but related stages.

First, police must collect the offender in their suspect pool, which means their dragnet needs to be cast wide enough to include the person they are hunting for. This information can come from members of the public or from databases and files maintained by law enforcement and other agencies (e.g., sex offender registries, jail booking records, department of motor vehicles files, etc.). While the collection stage is not unproblematic, police can always cast a wider suspect net. Indeed, the offender was in the suspect pool in all four of the crime series mentioned in the introduction to this chapter. The challenge is to avoid inappropriate exclusions. It has happened that a witness incorrectly described the race of the offender, resulting in a critical hole in the dragnet. To some degree this danger can be mitigated by thinking less in terms of elimination (short of exclusion by physical evidence or other incontrovertible means) and more in terms of prioritization.

Second, individuals should be prioritized and the suspect pool searched in the most efficient manner possible. Prioritization can occur through physical description, behavior, or geography. The process works best if the factors used to prioritize individuals are those readily available to investigators. For example, age, criminal record, and residential address are all easily accessible; information on clothing owned, personality disorders, and past residences are not.

Third, suspects must be evaluated in order to assess the likelihood of their involvement in the crime. Such evaluations can come from looking for opportunity, motive, and means. Police may also examine previous criminal records and modus operandi, composite sketches or forensic video evidence, alibis, and statements of family, friends, acquaintances, neighbors, or co-workers. If the crime is serious enough, the number of suspects manageable, and sufficient resources available, the assessment may creep into the "prove guilty" stage. Suspects will be interviewed, asked to provide physical evidence (e.g., fingerprints, DNA), and their photographs shown to victims or witnesses.

Suspect Prioritization

Important to the effective management of large volumes of investigative information are prioritization techniques, or optimal search strategies. These must be both valid (i.e., the correct individual is usually assigned a high priority) and useful (i.e., they employ observable criteria typically and reliably known to police during the investigation of unsolved crimes). There are various ways of prioritizing lists of suspects, but the major methods can be grouped into three categories: (1) physical description; (2) behavior; and (3) geography.

In some cases a surviving victim or witness may provide police with a physical description of an offender (e.g., white male, 30-40 years old, 5' 10" to 6', heavy-set, tattoo of red skull with "FTW" on a banner underneath, wearing a black leather jacket, black T-shirt, and blue jeans, and with the smell of liquor on his breath). While investigators can employ this information to prioritize suspects on their list, some of the descriptors are more useful than others. Unfortunately, little systematic research on eyewitness error patterns exists, making likelihood ratings for the different descriptive characteristics difficult to access accurately. Consequently, physical descriptions tend to be used more for elimination purposes.

Prioritization by behavior falls into the realm of what is called *behavioral analysis* or *psychological profiling*. Profiling can be general or specific. General profiles (sometimes referred to as statistical profiles) are summary descriptions of the type of person who commits a certain crime (e.g., child molestation). The prioritization criteria are the same for every crime in that group. For example, a study by the National Center for the Analysis of Violent Crime (NCAVC) found the typical serial arsonist was a young, white, middle-class male, nocturnal, and of average to above average intelligence (Sapp et al., 1994). More than 50 percent were labourers. Most had prior felony arrests and had been in county jails. Half of the offenders studied came from dysfunctional families, and many had histories of psychological problems.

The advantages of general profiles is that they are quick and easy to use and do not require a new, individualized analysis based on the specific crime in question. Their disadvantage is that they lack the precision of a profile constructed from that crime. To the degree that the sample on which the statistics are based is small or not representative of the overall population of relevant offenders, they may also be biased and inaccurate.

Specific profiles are developed from a detailed analysis of the crime under investigation. They are usually more accurate and contain more detail and a richer perspective. This approach attempts to determine the unknown offender's personality and other characteristics through an analysis of the characteristics of the crime scene. A crime-specific profile also typically suggests investigative strategies tailored to that crime and its investigation. Profiling requirements are information-intensive, perhaps because of the method's probabilistic nature. A profile can provide a variety of suggestions concerning offender characteristics, including likely age, race, sex, socioeconomic status, education level, marital status, employment background, criminal record particulars, psychiatric history, and military history. Crime-specific profiles require more work and can take time to prepare. Not every crime can be profiled.

Geography is the third method of suspect prioritization, and it also involves general and specific approaches. The general approach is based on the application of findings from journey-to-crime studies. Individuals who live near the scene of the crime are given higher priority than those residing farther away. There have been many such studies on the typical distance offenders travel to commit various crimes (see Rossmo, 2000, for a summary). Such information can be used as a guide for investigators in their search for an offender, because suspects can be prioritized within circles established from a journey-to-crime radius centered on the offense location. For example, the NCAVC study found that 20 percent of serial arsonists set fires within half a mile of their home, 50 percent within one mile, and 70 percent within two miles. The same concerns and limitations that apply to statistical profiles—a lack of representativeness and lack of precision—exist here.

Specific geographic analysis, more commonly known as geographic profiling, is based on an examination of the crime (or crime series) under investigation (Rossmo, 1997, 2000). Again, this approach requires more effort and time. Geographic profiling is discussed in more detail below.

Table 1 provides a schematic of the criminal investigative process. It is a simplification and is meant only to describe criminal investigations experiencing the problem of information overload. It certainly does not include every investigative approach, and some categories overlap. But within these limitations, the table may provide a useful framework for police detectives in developing strategies and assessing strengths and limitations in a particular investigation.

Problem-Solving Approach

Theory

Geographic profiling is based in the theoretical field of environmental criminology. Theory concerns itself with explanation and prediction, and much of criminological theory is naturally interested in why crimes happen and why people break the law. Environmental criminology, however, seeks to answer a different set of questions. Its focus is on why crime happens where and when it does—in other words, the explanation of crime patterns. Consequently, environmental criminology provides a rich mine of ideas of practical value for crime prevention and police operations. Three subareas are of particular importance to geographic profiling: rational choice, routine activity, and crime pattern theories.

Table 1
Criminal Investigative Process

Find Offender				Prove Guilt
Collect Suspects		Prioritize	Evaluate	Direct/Indirect Evidence
Public Tips Witnesses Informants Friends Family Neighbors	**Databases** Criminal Records Police Files DMV Other Agencies	Physical Description	Opportunity Motive Means	Witness
		Behavior • General • Specific	Modus Operandi Composite Sketch Video Alibi	Confession
		Geography • General • Specific	Suspect Interview Interviews of Family, Friends, and Neighbors	Physical Evidence

The *rational choice* perspective regards criminal choices and behavior as the result of a rational consideration of the costs, benefits, and efforts of other possible actions (Cornish & Clarke, 1986). This suggests that even the worst serial killer, with the most bizarre crime scene behavior, operates with a basic level of rationality. Indeed, criminals who behave irrationally are soon caught, so it is rare that they become serial offenders.

Routine activity theory states that in order for a contact predatory crime to happen, there must be an intersection in time and space between a motivated offender, a suitable target, and the absence of capable guardianship (Felson, 2002). In other words:

$$\text{crime} = (\text{offender} + \text{target} - \text{guardian}) \, (\text{place} + \text{time})$$

The routine activity approach is useful for understanding the circumstances surrounding a crime and the specific actions of the offender and the victim that led up to their encounter.

Crime pattern theory is key to geographic profiling. Much crime, especially violent crime, appears to be haphazard. But there is a rationality influencing where and when it happens and a logic to its geographic structure. Brantingham and Brantingham (1981) developed crime pattern theory—a model of crime site geometry—in which they postulate that crimes occur primarily in areas where the offender's awareness space intersects suitable target areas. An individual's awareness space is a direct product of his or her activity space, which in turn is constructed from one's home, workplace, recreational sites, and the travel routes between them. The relationship to routine activities is apparent. Suitable target areas are those with desirable targets and an acceptable risk level (as seen from the perspective of the offender).

Crime Sites

Crimes can involve more than one location. For example, a murder has an encounter, an attack, a murder, and a body disposal site. A bank robbery typically has only a single site, but if a stolen car is used, there can also be vehicle theft and drop sites. The various locations connected to a crime have different meanings and purposes for the offender. Multiple crime sites group together in various manners. The four different types of murder sites, for example, can cluster together in eight different combinations, ranging from one (every action happens in the same location) to four (every action happens in a different location) different sites. *Crime parsing* is the name given to breaking an offense down into its constituent locations and their combinations.

Hunting

The criminal hunt is made up of the offender's search for a target or victim and the attack. Searching may involve observing, casing, trespassing, prowling, and peeping. Criminals' activity spaces, in combination with how they hunt, determine the location and size of their hunting grounds. Thus criminal target patterns—the geography of crime sites—are influenced by the offender, the victim, and environmental variables. Several other factors are important considerations in the preparation of a geographic profile, including offense and offender type, neighborhood demographics, land use and zoning, physical and mental barriers, and the possibility of displacement.

In summary, crime site patterns are a function of the generating process and the background environment, the most important of which are:

- offender activity space—home, work, social activities, and connecting travel routes;

- hunting style—criminal search and attack methods;

- hunting ground—range and areas of criminal search; and

- target backdrop—distribution of potential targets or victims within the hunting ground.

Investigative Strategies

While this chapter is concerned with the process of suspect prioritization by geography, a complex serial crime investigation typically involves many facets. Depending on the circumstances of the case, other approaches may also be productive. A geographic profile can be the basis for several different investigative strategies, including:

- directing patrol saturation and surveillance efforts;

- focusing mail-outs and neighborhood notifications to obtain community information;

- establishing search boundaries for DNA dragnets;

- finding fugitive hiding locations;

- analyzing pay phone and cellular telephone locations in extortion and kidnapping investigations;

- determining probable body dump sites in missing person cases that are suspected homicides; and

- providing expert testimony and search warrant grounds under certain circumstances.

For additional details, see Rossmo (2000) and MacKay (1999).

Results

The accuracy of a specific geoprofile is determined by a measure known as the *hit score percentage*. It is equal to the area that has to be searched before the offender is located, divided by the total area covered by the crimes. For example, if the crimes are spread out over 10 square miles and the offender is found in the top one-half of a square mile, the hit score percentage is five percent (= 0.5/10). A recent review of now-solved operational cases from four different police agencies that provide geographic profiling services and research findings from Simon Fraser University produced a mean hit score percentage of 4.7 percent (standard deviation = 4.4%), and a median of 3.0 percent (N = 70 crime series, representing 1,426 crimes).

As previously discussed, there are many different suspect prioritization schemes. And it is a combination of prioritization methods, not any single method, that produces the optimal suspect search strategy. This is a basic feature of probability that underlies all prioritization schemes. Two examples illustrate the power of an integrated approach.

Operation Lynx

Operation Lynx—the investigation of five serial rapes in Leeds, Leicester, and Nottingham from 1982 to 1995—was the largest police manhunt in Britain since the Yorkshire Ripper inquiry. Detectives had obtained DNA scene evidence, victim descriptions of the offender, and a partial fingerprint. A search of the United Kingdom's national DNA databank failed to produce a match, and the partial print had too few characteristics for an Automated Fingerprint Identification System (AFIS) search. Police had connected a stolen vehicle (inside which was the owner's Visa card) with the first rape. This was also taken and fraudulently used in several locations around West Yorkshire. Combining the Leeds rape sites with the Visa fraud sites resulted in 20 unique locations upon which a geographic profile could be based.

Investigators wanted to manually search the West Yorkshire Constabulary fingerprint files for matches to the partial print but needed to prioritize this effort (West Yorkshire has a population of approximately two million). They used the search parameters of sex, race, ethnicity, age, criminal record, and residence area. A matching print was found in the second police station on the geographically prioritized list, and both DNA and a confession confirmed the person's guilt. At the time of the crimes the offender, Clive Barwell, was living in the top 3.0 percent (21 square miles) of the geoprofile. He pled guilty to four rape charges in 1999 and was sentenced to multiple life terms in prison.

Interestingly, one of the prioritization criteria—ethnicity—was incorrect. While Barwell spoke to his victims with a Scottish accent, this was a ruse, because he was actually English. His intention was to throw off the victims and, subsequently, the police. The fact that he was still apprehended illustrates the power of probability: a prioritization scheme does not have to be perfect (and rarely is in the real world), because other factors help to compensate for inaccuracies.

Project Loch Ness

Project Loch Ness was initiated by the Peel Regional Police to investigate a rape and 10 sexual assaults of young women in suburban Toronto. Detectives collected a total of 312 suspects from known sex offenders, public tips, and police records. A DNA scene sample was available from the rape, but testing every suspect was deemed too expensive. The detectives developed a prioritization and assessment scheme involving the following factors: composite sketch, uncorroborated alibi, initial interview, geographic profile, and psychological profile.

Of the 312 suspects, 144 were eliminated and the remaining 168 were grouped into three levels of priority. A match was obtained from the first batch of forensic samples submitted to the laboratory. Lee Marvin Payne was arrested in 1998 and subsequently pled guilty. He was first in the overall prioritization scheme. Based only on the geographic profile, Payne would have been sixth, with a hit score percentage of 1.9 percent as measured by suspects, and 2.2 percent as measured by area (0.03 square miles). The case was solved through DNA and a confession, but prioritizing suspects led to a quicker arrest, significant cost savings, and likely fewer victims.

Conclusion

Forst (2004) makes the point that "an unsolved crime is a problem" (267), and argues that even though the typical investigative process is reactive, not proactive, there is room for problem solving by police detectives (see also Eck, 1999). This can occur through a shift in focus from offenses to offenders and locations and by identifying patterns of criminal activity. By making proper and full use of modus operandi files and related police data sources, detectives can be more effective at both linking related crimes (thereby identifying crime series) and connecting crimes to offenders (particularly serial criminals). Geographic profiling provides one method of helping address the problem of information overload in serial crime investigations.

References

Abel, G.G., Mittelman, M.S., and J.V. Becker (1985). "Sexual Offenders: Results of Assessment and Recommendations for Treatment." In *Clinical Criminology: The Assessment and Treatment of Criminal Behaviour* 191-205. Toronto: MM Graphics.

Brantingham, P.J., and P.L. Brantingham (1981). *Environmental Criminology* (1991 reissue). Prospect Heights, IL: Waveland Press.

Clarke, R.V., and J.E. Eck (2003). *Become a Problem-Solving Crime Analyst: In 55 Small Steps*. London: Ad Hoc Publications.

Cornish, D.B., and R.V. Clarke (eds.) (1986). *The Reasoning Criminal: Rational Choice Perspectives on Offending*. New York: Springer-Verlag.

Eck, J.E. (1999). "Problem-Solving Detectives: Some Thoughts on Their Scarcity." *When the Heat's On*. Seattle: Seattle Police Department.

Felson, M. (2002). *Crime and Everyday Life,* Third Edition. Thousand Oaks, CA: Sage Publications.

Forst, B. (2004). "Problem-Oriented Criminal Investigation." In Q.C. Thurman and J. Zhao (eds.), *Contemporary Policing: Controversies, Challenges, and Solutions*. Los Angeles: Roxbury Publishing.

Klockars, C.B., and S.D. Mastrofski (eds.) (1991). *Thinking about Police: Contemporary Readings*, Second Edition. New York: McGraw-Hill.

MacKay, R.E. (1999). "Geographic Profiling: A New Tool for Law Enforcement." *The Police Chief*, Vol. LXI, No. 12:51-59.

Rossmo, D.K. (1997). "Geographic Profiling." In J.L. Jackson & D.A. Bekerian (eds.), *Offender Profiling: Theory, Research and Practice*. Chichester: John Wiley & Sons.

_____ (2000). *Geographic Profiling*. Boca Raton, FL: CRC Press.

Sapp, A.D., Huff, T.G., Gary, G.P., Icove, D.J., and P. Horbert (1994). *A Report of Essential Findings from a Study of Serial Arsonists*. Quantico, VA: National Center for the Analysis of Violent Crime.

Chapter 14
Problem Solving Terrorism Vulnerability

Les Poole

Introduction

A donkey cart, a mailbox, a garbage bin, a package delivered to the office, a letter, a suitcase, a car, a truck, an airplane, a subway carriage, a dog, or a human being can be harmless objects in themselves. Yet recently each has been used by terrorists as a container or projectile that caused human suffering, injury, or death. Moreover, the presence of these items in everyday life in Western civilization is as natural and unobserved as the glass in our windows.

Domestic preparedness encompasses two interrelated concerns: first, raising the awareness of police and other emergency services and the communities they serve to the potential of a terrorist threat without creating alarm and unduly increasing the level of fear; and second, enhancing the capability of these groups to respond most effectively in the event of a threat being realized and to secure safety for everyone. This chapter aims to address both of those issues and focuses on two primary police functions—the prevention of crime and the protection of life and property.

Background

The targets threatened, damaged, or destroyed by terrorist attacks have been as diverse as their sources of origin. The attackers are equally varied in terms of where they come from, their causes, and the purposes of their actions. Attacks have come from both in and out of the country. With such a variety of possible sources, targets, and deliverers, the task of policing is complex and difficult. Consequently, the task may seem overwhelming, if not unproductive and of doubtful practical value.

A recent survey undertaken by the International Association of Chiefs of Police found that 33 percent of members felt somewhat unprepared and 38 percent not at all prepared to prevent a terrorist act. In responding to a terrorist act, 31 percent felt somewhat unprepared and 13 percent not at all prepared. The level of preparedness of agencies to deal with weapons of mass destruction and terrorist attacks also was low. Many of the reasons cited were related to funding and equipment, but others were linked to inadequate training and inadequate collaboration efforts. These results are in marked contrast to the chiefs' views when they were asked to consider levels of preparedness for dealing with natural disaster and barricaded suspect/hostage incidents in which only 15 percent and 13 percent, respectively, felt somewhat or not at all prepared to deal with them.

This chapter seeks to convince police agencies and municipal authorities that something very practical can be done without bankrupting the local budget. The terrorist threat has proven far less reliable in its recurrence. Terrorism demands preparation for future unforeseen circumstances and challenges the police to respond in similar fashion through contingency planning. The goal is a collaborative partnership initiative that focuses on analysis of the problem, the will to address it, and good local communication between police and other involved parties. Much of this must be focused on the efforts of local law enforcement agencies that play a crucial role in developing plans, gathering intelligence, and dealing with "live" incidents.

Problem-Solving Approach

Drawing public attention through the media to imprecise threats does nothing to reduce fear of terrorist attack—it just makes people uneasy. In the same way we know that thousands die and are injured every year in traffic accidents and gun-related incidents, we tend to assume that "it won't happen to us." Because of the lack of clarity about targets or the method of delivery, most people go about their daily lives assuming that they are relatively safe from harm. Thankfully, they are usually right, and that is how humans have ordered their lives for centuries.

However, public safety agencies cannot be indifferent to this information and have a real need to prepare for these contingencies and "what if" scenarios. The task requires careful thought, considerable foresight, and some risk-taking. Whatever the incident, emergency services will be first on the scene. They will be the first responders and could be the targets of secondary attacks. If the threat is taken seriously or the terrorist act is carried out, it will again be the police who have to arrange for evacuation, cordoning, access to the site, and preservation of the scene for forensic examination. It is with those concerns in mind that the following ideas are presented.

A word of warning: the involvement of the community in partnerships needs to be done with sensitivity and care so as to reduce fear and alarm and to offer honest reassurance. The purpose is to increase the public's state of alertness and vigilance and to help the public feel better prepared and less helpless in these disturbing situations and their aftermath. Alarming the public or making people more fearful will do more harm than good. Despite that caveat, police must make a real effort to involve the community. They can help the police with their knowledge, experience, and capacity to respond. They can also supply the vital intelligence needed to combat these potential threats to the security of our local environment.

Step 1: Identifying Specific Targets

Using the SARA model (Scan–Analyze–Respond–Assess), the first stage is to scan the local environment and to prepare a list of potential targets. Here we must identify the specific criteria for targets in order to be able to prioritize planning and follow-up in the analysis stage. The police agency has to ask certain questions in the light of its own and others' experience. Access to any community survey information that indicates specific fears in relation to terrorism should be noted, but such information need not be actively solicited from the community. This process should be focused on the police agency itself and on any other agencies with which it collaborates and shares information with regard to local domestic preparedness.

Relevant questions to be asked include:

- What type of incident or terrorist threat would create major disruption in your community?

- What events are likely to result in extensive loss of life or serious injuries?

- What type of incident or terrorist threat is likely to create fear among the residents and business community?

- What events are likely to have major impact on the local community?

- What incident or terrorist threat is likely to result in major economic damage to your community—whether financial, business, or political—or would seriously affect commuter interests?

Any local, state, or federal intelligence or threat assessments that identify specific sites as potential targets also need to be carefully considered in prioritizing subsequent decisions. In collaboration with this wider police community and key agency personnel, a local list should be drawn up. A brainstorm activity is an ideal method of determining this information. Similarly, a broad range of terrorist threats should be considered—including physical threats such as bombs, explosives, and mortars, and potential chemical and biological weapons or "dirty bombs." The following list of potential targets is by no means exhaustive. The final list will be dictated by local high-profile utilities, facilities, and buildings; geography; demography; and other local concerns.

- Schools (preschools, K-12, and college/university campuses)
- Federal/state/municipal buildings and government offices; state/town hall; gubernatorial election/acceptance speeches; security details
- Polling stations on election days
- Hospitals; daycare centers; nursing homes
- Military facilities
- Armories
- Courts and high-profile court buildings
- Energy sites
- Water treatment facilities, reservoirs, and dams
- Food processing plants
- Airports and bus or ferry terminals
- Railway stations; mass transit systems generally
- Convention centers; other locations where large gatherings are anticipated; state fairs; election meetings
- National monuments
- Places of worship and religious institutions
- Sports arenas; amusement parks; museums; zoos; theaters; other sites of major public gatherings
- Shopping malls—major department stores; major chains that may be particularly vulnerable
- Commercial key assets and office buildings
- Hotels and business meeting centers
- Busy public parks
- Bridges and tunnels
- Large factories and office buildings
- Hotels

- Libraries

- Environmental/ecological/animal rights targets

- Major routes in and out of cities

- Major truck parks and truck stops

- U.S. mailboxes and mail sorting centers—USPS, FedEx, UPS, DHL

- Garbage containers

Examples of some of the most serious terrorist activities that have taken place in some of the locations listed above are Oklahoma City (1995), World Trade Center (1993, 2001), the Tokyo subway system (1995), and Heathrow Airport, London (1994). Environmental, eco-terrorist, and animal rights groups also have successfully targeted diverse enterprises, causing millions of dollars in damage and injuries, e.g., car dealers selling expensive vehicles (SUVs); logging trucks burnt in a national forest; banks funding activities of laboratories; and establishments considered by the groups to be detrimental to their cause.

A critical concern of police officials throughout this process is to preserve the safety of all members of the community, including the first responders, and to raise awareness of possible threats and safe responses. Every effort needs to be taken to ensure public safety.

Step 2: Analyzing the Information

Answering the questions posed earlier will provide the identifying criteria to determine the focus on a list of local priorities and enable the information to be analyzed. A decision then has to be made within the agency as to where police efforts should first be directed. This involves drawing up a list of sites that terrorists might target and then prioritizing them. At this point there should be some clear indications of the most vulnerable areas, and careful consideration should be given to the extent to which public awareness can be increased without creating a greater sense of vulnerability.

The list should be linked to other agencies, hospitals, businesses, and organizations that should be contacted in order to enhance domestic preparedness and community safety and that could directly assist in coping with an incident. Once prioritized, the list should be worked through until proper steps are in place in all the locations of concern. For example, at sites where large numbers of people gather, such as local places of worship, there is a need to consult with the management or religious leader to establish any plans they may have in place for evacuation and find out how they manage security at their events. If security is the responsibility of an outside contractor, then this contractor must also become part of the contact process.

If the sites are educational, links need to be made to the establishment itself, the principal, and any security staff or on-site police agency in order to review the arrangements. Relevant questions here relate to security on the site, closed-circuit television, and details of designated staff able to deal with serious problems. This stage also involves identifying details of partners who need to be contacted and making initial contacts with those concerned to gather additional information that will provide the basic data for a contingency plan, information sharing, and increased awareness.

Typical partnerships include other local government agencies—health, education, and public works; other law enforcement agencies—federal, state, and local—with whom terrorist intelligence is shared; and other emergency services when there is a need to verify communications compatibility and resolve the question of who has overall control at the scene. Other partners might be local community organizers who are eager to assist these police initiatives. In the purely local context, business owners, utility owners, shopkeepers, or security staff can effectively work with the police and preserve their own interests. The local press may also have a role in immediately notifying people via radio or television of areas to be avoided or precautions to be taken. The emphasis must remain on increasing awareness and improving alertness, yet acting calmly.

The final element of the partnership is to cement the relationship between the police and the communities they serve. The public remains the best possible source of intelligence on terrorism as well as other criminal matters. Any steps to nurture their involvement on such an important issue can have positive dividends for enhancing the police response to terrorist attack. Personal contact and communication in this area will benefit both police and the public.

Step 3: Planning a Response

Responses will depend on whether the incident actually takes place or is a hoax. In the case of the former, there are questions of evidence gathering and scene preservation that are absent in the hoax situation. In both instances, plans for cordoning off, evacuating, and searching are likely to be similar. If the sites selected are the responsibility of the police agency, every effort should be made to obtain a blueprint or photographs of the premises or at least a detailed floor plan or map, preferably electronic, that can be stored at the police facility.

There are many examples of sites where political appointments of state and local officials in government buildings take place with police responsibility for the entire security detail, but where no record of the plans of the locations are registered with police. This is a very shortsighted approach. What was learned from Columbine should bring home the need to have detailed plans of such facilities. When considering the diverse nature of terrorism, it is even more critical. What sort of information is required?

- Access—exits and windows—ocation

- Staircases, escalators, elevators—location and areas they give access to

- Rooms, size and access, type of activity conducted there

- Heating/air conditioning/ventilator systems—points of access and delivery

- Position of utility controls and extent—water, electricity, gas

- Alarm systems and sprinklers

- Surveillance equipment, CCTV, positions of cameras and monitors, and access points to tape location

- Storage of hazardous substances

- Radio reception; cell-phone repeaters

- Key availability; phone numbers of key holders

- Points of contact for relevant personnel and ability to update data

In the event of a terrorist or other serious incident, this information will provide the appropriate framework in which police can respond most effectively; isolate, contain, or evacuate the site; and advise others of its safety. It is invaluable to any SWAT team commander who has to cope with this type of incident. Without it, the location is likely to be a mystery to the officers when they arrive at a time when any delay is critical.

The follow-up stage involves establishing a joint plan with the agencies concerned to address the potential threat and to work jointly toward producing a clear and simple plan to deal promptly with any threat and to evacuate the area as quickly as possible if disruption and injury follow an actual attack. A clear plan should be devised to respond to the potential threat and any resulting chaos. This brief article cannot deal with the myriad of circumstances possible in police responses to terrorism. Many links with other law enforcement agencies will enable smaller agencies to develop expertise in this area. More plans are continuously being put into place. The Federal Emergency Management Agency also has expertise in emergency planning and evacuation procedures. Major sites (e.g., nuclear power plants) should have potential citizen evacuation routes mapped in advance and distributed to the community as necessary with maximum media cooperation.

Particularly vulnerable without a comprehensive contingency plan are shopping malls and large spaces where many people gather and the threat of bombs or similar devices is real. Even dealing with hoaxes may require search and evacuation plans. The following examples relate to potential threats that affect busy public places. The precautions and planning are essential in responding to potential threats.

Garbage Containers Outside Vulnerable Premises, such as government offices, military recruiting offices, banks, and high-profile commercial operations, have been used to conceal packaged devices capable of inflicting great harm. Containers should be emptied at least twice a day on an unpredictable schedule. Special care should be taken in removing them; public works employees involved must be warned and trained to respond appropriately. Specific information or events at identified locations should result in sealing or removing the containers, perhaps even permanently. Blast-proof containers are available but are expensive. Boxes for U.S. mail may fall into this category.

Letter/parcel/Incendiary Devices are usually designed to explode when opened. Review any obviously vulnerable places, and establish a contingency plan with business owners/managers for dealing with them. Postal staff are particularly susceptible to this type of attack, and local union branches are likely to be supportive partners in addressing this. All mailroom staff who regularly open or handle incoming mail need appropriate advice and training. Advice on the location or relocation of mailrooms in business areas is also relevant here. A plan for evacuating all or part of a building is necessary, including specifics about areas to be cordoned off and the appropriate agency to be called, for example, the Bureau of Alcohol, Tobacco, Firearms and Explosives. Packages that may contain toxic substances (such as anthrax) require development of an appropriate plan with the business owners/managers concerned and an agreed-upon evacuation process.

Bomb Calls, Hoaxes, or Suspected Unexploded Devices also require attention. For example, in shopping malls there is a need for an evacuation plan for the entire mall, a search plan, a contact point, details of those in charge, and key holders' details. The information referred to earlier about points of access, utilities, and so forth is fundamental to preparing a plan to deal with serious incidents in a mall. Partners include mall security, business owners, shopkeepers, and office managers. The options here involve providing advice on crime prevention and the use of CPTED-trained staff.

Evacuation plans for shopping malls should focus initially on 10 key stores that are likely to remain in the location for the long term. Creating a cascading notification system, or phone chain, for evacuation in the event of a threat or after an incident is highly effective, the first 10 stores all contacting 10 other stores each until all premises are covered. Using this technique, British police have managed to evacuate more than 500 stores in less than 10 minutes very effectively, securing the area, and avoiding further injuries.

In addition to the plan for the entire mall, there should be both a search plan and an evacuation plan for large stores and other businesses within the mall. The following specific advice on bomb searches can be given to partners, such as:

1. Search the most vulnerable areas first.

2. Search outside buildings to which public has easy access.

3. Search lobbies and entrances to offices, plants, or depots to which the public normally have access.

4. Search basements, bathrooms, boiler rooms, and utility areas with easy access from public areas.

5. Working areas where the public is normally excluded are generally less vulnerable to outside attack, but beware of unescorted visitors.

6. In the event of an exploded device, searchers should take special care that there is not a secondary device in close proximity to the first that is designed to injure emergency responders.

Step 4: Assessing Effectiveness

Contingency plans must be readily available at all times to shift commanders and, in some cases, dispatchers. Plans locked in the car of someone on vacation are useless. The plans also need to be reviewed on a regular basis, biannually at least, and key contacts should be in frequent communication with their local department.

The normal criteria for assessing problem-solving plans are not readily transferable to this area of increasing domestic preparedness. The questions of "Did it work?" "Have we fixed the problem?" and "Have our goals been met?" are difficult to answer. The factors in this equation are less tangible than statistics about reducing crime or improving road safety. If there is a better-informed and aware police agency and community as a result of these initiatives, then some fear and insecurity will have been reduced. Like intelligence gathering, this is a leap of faith to meet the ultimate objective of delivering quality service to our communities and achieving a reduced sense of vulnerability from terrorist attack.

Plans can be tested in the same way as a fire drill to establish effectiveness. Many agencies run mock scenarios with partners and emergency services to test the effectiveness of the plans. One or two drills at identified sites can show both the strengths and weaknesses of the plan and lead to substantial improvement. The plan is a form of public safety insurance against unknown contingencies that in the last resort can save lives of both police officers and people in the communities they serve. One can no longer assume that "it won't happen to us." To have no plan is unacceptable, perhaps even negligent. Having a plan is a positive step, but it needs to be a crisis management plan that is a "live" working document, regularly updated with current information. Clearly, it is preferable that the plan be tested in practice rather than be found wanting in the ultimate test.

Conclusion

While this approach to terrorism is not cost-neutral, its cost is minimal compared to expensive training and equipment. It embraces the need for police to interact and communicate with their various communities with its positive rewards. It also addresses a real need to prepare a comprehensive list of threats and local vulnerabilities. This could form the nucleus of any national database for the United States, with maximum involvement of local law enforcement agencies. The approach challenges some established organizational police practices by creating contingency plans to deal with a specific crime, and encourages a preventive, proactive approach to domestic preparedness rather than a reactive one.

If this approach increases the awareness of police officers, their supervisors, and the community to possible terrorist threats and helps them be prepared for terrorism in all its guises, some progress will have been made. Public alarm must be avoided, yet people need to think twice about seeing an apparently abandoned suitcase and doing nothing about it. In other parts of the world doing so at times has had very costly consequences.

References

Bankson, R. (2003). "Terrorism: National in Scope, Local in Execution." *Community Links* 8:3-4. Washington, DC: COPS Office, U.S. Department of Justice.

_____ (2003). "An Executive Perspective on Terrorism." *Community Links* 8:10-11. Washington, DC: COPS Office, U.S. Department of Justice.

_____ (2003). "Addressing the Fear of Crime—Mobilizing Against Terrorism." *Community Links* 8:12-13. Washington, DC: COPS Office, U.S. Department of Justice.

British Council for Offices (1993). *Bombs and Terrorist Threats in Office Buildings and Business Space*.

Chapman, R., and M. Scheider. (Fall 2002) "Community Policing: Now More Than Ever." *On the Beat* No. 19. Washington, DC: COPS Office, U.S. Department of Justice. Available at: http://www.cops.usdoj.gov/default.asp?item=716.

Chapman, R., S. Baker, V. Bezdikian, P. Cammarata, D. Cohen, N. Leach, A. Schapiro, M. Scheider, R. Varano, and R. Boba (April 2002). "Local Law Enforcement Responds to Terrorism: Lessons in Prevention and Preparedness." *COPS Innovations: a Closer Look*. Washington, DC: COPS Office, U.S. Department of Justice. Available at: http://www.cops.usdoj.gov/mime/open.pdf?Item=296

Dunn, M. (2003). "Assessing Threats Directed at School Facilities." *Law and Order*. Available at: http://www.hendonpub.com/lawmag/swatroom.htm.

Office of Safe and Drug-Free Schools (2003). "Crisis Planning Resources." Washington, DC: U.S. Department of Education. Available at: http://www.ed.gov/admins/lead/safety/emergencyplan/index.html.

Giannone, D., and R.A. Wilson (2003). "The Cat Eye Program: Enlisting Community Members in the Fight Against Terrorism." *The Police Chief* (March):37-38.

Gorman, S. (2003). "Homeland Security Chair Calls for Restraint in First Responder Spending." *National Journal* (November 14).

International Association of Chiefs of Police (2003). "Homeland Security Preparedness Survey." *The Police Chief* (August). Available at http://www.theiacp.org/documents/pdfs/WhatsNew/ACF187C.pdf.

Lyall, S. (2003). "The World: IRA to Al Qaeda; Where Threats Are Always Orange." *New York Times* May 25: section 4, p. 7.

Miller, J., M. Stone, and C. Mitchell (2002). *The Cell—Inside the 9/11 Plot*. New York: Hyperion.

The White House (February 2003). *The National Strategy for the Physical Protection of Critical Infrastructures and Key Assets*. Washington, DC: Author. Available at: http://www.whitehouse.gov/pcipb/physical.html

National Governors' Association Center for Best Practices (2001). *Domestic Preparedness Checklist*. Available at: http://www.nga.org/cda/files/DomPrepChecklist.pdf.

Olin, W.R. (2002). "Why Traditional Law Enforcement Methods Cannot Win the War on Terrorism." *The Police Chief* Vol. 69, No. 11:27-31.

Online Support for Bomb Threat Response Planning Tool. See http://www.threatplan.org.

Samuel, J., Jr. (2003). "Building Partnerships between Private-Sector Security and Public-Sector Police: IACP President's Message." *The Police Chief* (September).

Sanchez, T. (2003). "High-Tech Crisis Plans—Tools for School Safety." *The Police Chief* (April).

Wadman, R.C. (1988). Trends in American Policing." *Journal of International Criminal Justice* 1:3.

Section V

Problem Solving in the Twenty-First Century

Chapter 15

Limitations, Challenges, and the Future of Police Problem Solving

Keith Ikeda

Introduction

Public safety has come a long way in the area of police problem solving. There are numerous documented examples of successful problem-solving projects across the United States found on the Internet and in a number of books and publications. These projects range from dealing with crime-infested housing projects to panhandling on public streets. In fact, it seems that problem-solving approaches to almost every policing problem have been documented. Problem solving has proven to be highly effective in reducing targeted crime, reducing targeted calls for service, and resolving community concerns.

Even so, some might say that we still have a long way to go. For starters, the majority of police agencies in the United States do not have formal problem-solving programs. Random patrol, rapid response, and investigative follow-ups are the standard patrol strategies for most police agencies. A formalized and coordinated problem-solving approach is not the tool of choice at the line level or throughout many public safety agencies.

This chapter examines the benefits and limitations of police problem solving, the challenges we will face in overcoming those limitations, and what it will take to support and sustain such an approach in the future.

Benefits

What are the advantages of implementing problem-solving strategies? How is it different from what police are currently doing?

As documented in this book, police problem solving is highly effective at reducing targeted calls for service, targeted crimes, and reducing community problems and concerns. Currently most police agencies react to calls for service and attempt to address each incident or case through documentation and enforcement efforts. If an arrest or enforcement is not possible, the incident or case is deactivated and the police wait for the next call for service. Even if an arrest is made, the case may end without determining other responses with regard to location, victim, and other contributing factors. For example, if police make a drug-dealing arrest, they may simply focus on the arrest and prosecution. With an arrest there comes the assumption that the problem is solved, without assessing whether this action has made a difference in the problem. Usually the drug dealer is replaced with another drug dealer because the demands for the drugs and the location where drugs can be sold have not been addressed. Problem solving expands the responses rather than relying solely on enforcement efforts.

Problem solving employs effective strategies to reduce calls for service. An example in which problem solving can make a difference involves police response to traffic accidents. Currently many police agencies document an accident in report form and issue a citation. Using a problem-solving approach, the police would identify their most accident-prone areas, analyze the contributing factors, and then respond with a well-rounded approach that combines engineering, education, and enforcement. After a time, there would be an assessment of the effectiveness that the new approach achieved in reducing accidents. If the responses did not have an impact, the process would start over again until the desired results are achieved.

Problem solving uses self-directed, uncommitted time more effectively by directing efforts toward targeted problems. By focusing on and reducing targeted problems, the police can have a direct and significant impact on the law enforcement workload. This problem-solving strategy is far better than relying on traditional strategies and hoping the problems will be reduced.

Implementing problem-solving strategies does not require additional personnel or increases in the budget. Problem solving is a systematic process that identifies the scope of the problem then analyzes the problem from all angles, including identification of the stakeholders affected by the problem and of the outside resources needed to resolve the problem. The stakeholders will become involved if they believe the strategies employed will be effective in resolving problems. There are many ways to acquire outside resources available to police that may have never been considered in the past. There are private and public grants, community endowment funds, volunteer organizations, nonprofit organizations, insurance companies, homeowners' associations, schools, parent organizations, sports organizations, interest-based organizations, faith-based groups, fraternal organizations, businesses, business organizations, and chamber of commerce groups willing to provide personnel, financial, and other resources for resolving problems.

Effective problem solving requires close working relationships with other police agencies, service agencies, community groups, and stakeholders. This coordinated community response has been instrumental in addressing domestic violence, sex crimes, child protection, and adult protection. These working relationships add resources and expertise and facilitate the coordination of roles and responsibilities to appropriate agencies, groups, or individuals. Working together develops a coordinated and seamless response in which all aspects of the problem are addressed and nothing falls through the cracks.

Police agencies can promote a positive image by publishing their problem-solving efforts. They can work with the media to develop in-depth public reports. Police can supplement the media's basic crime reports with information for the community informing them how to protect themselves from becoming victims and what resources and services are available to them. Requests for information from people who may have witnessed or have been victimized by crime also may be made. In the past, the police have tended to reply only to media requests for information regarding high-profile cases. The typical release was a brief set of facts of the case, and media questions often were answered with "no comment." The police have improved relationships with the media, and now their public information officers routinely address the media during critical incidents, high-profile cases, and positive police interaction stories. Like it or not, the majority of information the community receives regarding their police agency comes from the media. Developing a positive working relationship with the media will showcase to the community a professional and committed police department.

The last benefit cannot easily be measured with statistics. This is the sense of pride and satisfaction experienced by police officers and staff at being able to make a positive difference. Communities by and large have overwhelming support and respect for their police. Increasing the positive contacts with the community and having police officers who are approachable and friendly builds trust and opens communications with citizens. Being a role model and taking the time to get to know the people you serve creates positive relationships. Helping others and making a community a safer and better place to live is immensely rewarding. After all, isn't this the reason most people become police officers?

Limitations

So if problem solving is so effective, why aren't more police agencies practicing this approach?

Police agencies already use problem-solving strategies in a limited scope through law enforcement. However, expanding and formalizing the problem-solving process may be viewed as something new. A natural human instinct is to view change with a healthy dose of skepticism and resistance. Problem solving has long been recognized as a core component of a more radical style of policing known as community policing. Both critics and proponents of community policing might agree that community policing represents a departure from a more reactive, traditional approach that has been prevalent for much of the last century in American policing. To the extent that some agencies cling to a "just the facts, ma'am" policing culture, both problem solving and community policing represent dramatic changes.

Most police organizations probably lack the systems and support for effective problem solving. Many times the hiring, evaluation, training, promotion, recognition, and reward systems of an organization do not support a problem-solving approach. These systems may reward the "status quo" while penalizing problem-solving efforts. The command staff and mid-line supervisors play an important role in the success of changes, such as the implementation of a problem-solving philosophy as explained earlier in Timothy Oettmeier's chapter. If they are not committed to problem solving, acceptance of the approach will not occur in the ranks. In turn, officers will not risk annoying their supervisors. Supervisors should practice situational leadership and learn how to practice a participative management style when problem solving. They need to feel comfortable with not having to know all the answers. Their role is to facilitate and support the line officers through the problem-solving process.

Effective problem solving takes more time, effort, teamwork, coordination, cooperation, and participation by all of the stakeholders. Officers must take additional measures beyond responding to a call and writing a report. They must work together to identify and analyze problems. Responses are implemented in a planned and coordinated manner. Officers must change the way they use their self-directed time. Their time becomes directed to implement the responses. Officers must be able to work with the stakeholders to get their cooperation, participation, and support. The officer's role changes from an authoritarian role to a facilitator role. This aspect is one of the most difficult for the police. The police are more comfortable giving directives, commands, and orders, which they expect to be followed without deviation. In contrast, problem solving places them in a position to try to obtain voluntary compliance.

Problem solving has to be adopted universally within an organization if it is to succeed. It also must be applied globally to the range of problems that will challenge the agency in its daily operations. These challenges will take many forms that traditional policing might view as outside the responsibility of the police to affect. But these same conditions, such as alcohol and drug abuse, overcrowding, unemployment, urban decay, lack of education, and lack of parental control, contribute to crime problems that result in calls for policing services. Most police officers are quick to say that they are not social workers, surrogate parents, teachers, ministers, data entry clerks, or community leaders. But effective problem solving requires police and citizens to assume all of those roles and more. Root causes that fuel crime problems must be addressed at some level—and not just crimes that are the symptoms of larger issues—if public safety agencies want to make a difference in their communities. Cleaning up neighborhoods, addressing alcohol and drug abuse, assisting with educational and employment opportunities, and helping youth to develop into healthy, responsible adults will reduce crime, promote public safety, and lead to the development of civic pride.

Challenges

Are these limitations insurmountable? Are there ways to minimize the turmoil and resistance to change?

The first challenge is to encourage police agencies to have an open perspective for learning and evaluating problem-solving approaches. There are a number of problem-solving training programs available through the Federal Law Enforcement Training Center (FLETC), the Regional Community Policing Institutes, police training organizations, and private consultants. Every police department should consider sending key staff members to a problem-solving training program. In addition, departments should ask each of their employees to learn about local problem-solving efforts, around the state, and around the country. Published literature on problem solving is available through the Office of Community Oriented Policing Services (COPS), the Police Executive Research Forum (PERF), various police and sheriff organizations, the Internet, and a variety of books and publications. Contacting those who have used problem solving and then sharing that information throughout the department is recommended.

There must be commitment and support for problem solving throughout an entire organization starting from the agency head on down to the front office staff. Developing a dialogue within the department on the benefits and barriers of problem solving would be a good start. Doing so can help to identify and then conquer the concerns of departmental personnel with implementing a problem-solving approach.

Agencies adopting a problem-solving approach will want to obtain a commitment from every department member to give his or her best effort in problem solving. They also will need to work together to develop clear steps to be taken to implement problem solving and then identify the roles, responsibilities, and expectations of every level within the department toward this effort. In turn, the department's hiring, evaluation, training, promotion, recognition, and reward systems will have to be amended to ensure that problem solving is supported. All of this will involve training department personnel in enhancing their communication, facilitation, and teamwork skills, and learning collaboration methods. In addition, training command staff and mid-line supervisors in strategic planning, organizational change, and executive management is crucial.

Checking in with each level of the department to assess how well the problem-solving process is being implemented is also important. It is to be expected that whenever implementing major change, things get worse before they get better. There is a learning curve that needs to occur. Staying the course and allowing time for staff to become proficient and comfortable with these new tasks are components of the process.

This approach also includes involving the community and listening to what they identify as their police-related issues and concerns. Here many of the issues that can be expected to arise concern quality-of-life issues such as noise complaints, residential traffic complaints, people not cleaning up after their dogs and allowing them to run around unleashed, and kids loitering. The community has an active role in identifying and solving problems.

Departments should seek a coordinated community response group with other police agencies, service agencies, community groups, and stakeholders. After identifying the common problems that these groups might be interested in examining, agencies should develop operational protocols to maximize efficiencies with the expertise and experience of the group.

The final challenge to be met is *patience*. In police organizations, change is evolutionary, not revolutionary. There is a history, tradition, and pride in most police agencies of providing outstanding protection and service to their communities. The culture of policing will not change until policing personnel are convinced that change is in the best interests of the department.

The Future of Police Problem Solving

As stated in the first page of this chapter, police problem solving has come a long way. But challenges remain. The police profession has a long history of being progressive and doing the right thing. The future of police problem solving depends on each and every employee. There are many benefits for doing so on both a professional and personal level. Given a choice, most officers would choose being effective over ineffective, doing the right thing over the way it always has been done, and making a positive difference beyond just being on the job. Police officers must support each other in providing the highest level of service for their communities. People may have faith in the leaders of the police profession to continue to seek to improve their services, security, safety, and quality of life for the communities they serve. We have a bright future.

About the Authors

José M. Docobo is a colonel with the Hillsborough County Sheriff's Office in Tampa, Florida. He has more than 23 years of law enforcement experience and has worked in most administrative and operational assignments. Colonel Docobo earned a bachelor's degree in education (1980) from the University of South Florida. He is also a graduate of the Secret Service Dignity Protection Course, the FBI National Academy, and the Harvard University Senior Executive Program. He is currently enrolled in the master's degree in Homeland Security Program at the Naval Post-Graduate College.

Brian Forst is professor of justice, law and society at the School of Public Affairs, American University. He was a researcher for the U.S. President's Commission on an All-Volunteer Armed Force in 1968-1970 and a fellow at the Massachusetts Institute of Technology in 1970-1971. Then, following a distinguished 20-year career in the nonprofit research world, including positions as research director first at the Institute for Law and Social Research (1977-1985) and then the Police Foundation (1985-1989), returned to higher education in 1989. He was on the faculty of the George Washington University (1989-1992) prior to joining the faculty at American University. He is author of several books, including *Errors of Justice: Nature, Sources and Remedies* (Cambridge University Press, 2004); *The Privatization of Policing: Two Views* (Georgetown University Press, 1999) with Peter Manning; and *Power in Numbers* (John Wiley & Sons, 1987), among others. His research on prosecution, policing and deterrence is cited extensively by scholars of criminal justice and public policy. His current research focuses on the prevention of terrorism, errors of justice, the privatization and civilianization of policing, the logic of criminal investigation, and communitarian approaches to policing and prosecution. He was awarded the School of Public Affairs' Bernard H. Ross Teaching Excellence Award in 2002. Dr. Forst holds bachelor's and master's degrees from the University of California at Los Angeles, and a Ph.D. from the George Washington University.

Steve Griffith is the executive director of the Advanced Law Enforcement Training Center in San Marcos, Texas. He holds a master's degree in criminal justice from Sam Houston State University and a bachelor's degree in business administration from the University of Houston. He has 26 years of experience in law enforcement, including 16 years as chief of police.

Carl W. Hawkins Jr. is a major with the Hillsborough County Sheriff's Office in Tampa, Florida. He has more than 29 years of law enforcement experience at the sheriff's office and has worked in most administrative and operational assignments. Major Hawkins earned a Ph.D. in public administration (1982), a master's degree in criminal justice (1977) from Nova Southeastern University (Ft. Lauderdale, Florida) and a bachelor's degree in criminal justice (1974) from the University of South Florida. In 1996 he was awarded a community policing fellowship at the National Center for State, Local, and International Law Enforcement Training of the Federal Law Enforcement Training Center in Glynco, Georgia. He has published more than 10 articles and research reports in various books and periodicals. Major Hawkins teaches in the Graduate Criminology Program at the University of South Florida, the Criminology Program at the University of Tampa, and the Law Enforcement Executive Program at North Carolina State University. His research interests include community policing, leadership, future trends, and controversial issues in policing.

Lucy Edwards Hochstein is assistant professor of criminal justice at Radford University. She earned her Ph.D. in political science from Washington State University, where she focused on public administration issues. Her research interests include criminal justice program evaluation, formal interagency collaborations, public-private partnerships addressing community issues, elder abuse, and the role of advocates in the criminal justice system and has published several articles in refereed journals and books.

Keith Ikeda is the chief of the Basalt, Colorado, Police Department. Prior to this he served as the assistant chief of operations for the Aspen Police Department (1994-2001), where he implemented the principles and practices of community-oriented policing. He holds a bachelor's degree in psychology from the University of Washington. Ikeda has more than 20 years of law enforcement experience working with the National Park Service, Pitkin County Sheriff's Department, Kirkland Police Department, Aspen Police Department, and the Basalt Police Department. He is a trainer for the Federal Law Enforcement Training Center and the Colorado Regional Community Policing Institute in the areas of community policing, domestic violence, ethics and integrity, and effective policing problem solving.

J.D. Jamieson holds a Ph.D. in criminal justice from Sam Houston State University and has experience in the U.S. Army Counterintelligence Corps and law enforcement in Louisiana. He has been a faculty member for 18 years in the Department of Criminal Justice at Texas State University in San Marcos, Texas. He is currently assisting the ALERRT Center with feedback data processing and analysis as part of an ongoing attempt to measure first responder training effectiveness.

David Mueller is assistant professor of criminal justice at Boise State University. He received a Ph.D. in political science from Washington State University in 2001. His research interests include juvenile crime and violence, school-based delinquency prevention, and program evaluation. His latest publications include *Criminal Justice Case Briefs: Significant Cases in Juvenile Justice* (with Craig Hemmens and Benjamin Steiner, Roxbury, 2004); "So How Was Your Conference? Panel Chairs' Perceptions of the 2003 ACJS Meeting in Boston," *Journal of Criminal Justice Education* (2004) (with Andrew Giacomazzi and James Wada); and "School Shootings and the Man-Bites-Dog Criterion of Newsworthiness," *Youth Violence and Juvenile Justice* (2003) (with Dr. Richard Lawrence).

Timothy N. Oettmeier is in his 30th year of serving the public as a member of the Houston Police Department, where he serves as an Executive Assistant Chief of Police assigned to Professional Standards Command. His direct responsibilities include managing and administering the internal affairs division, the inspections division, and the office of inspector general. He has worked in a variety of assignments during his career, including serving as the chief of staff for the field operations command, the department's director of training, and as the city's inspector general for several years. He received his Ph.D. in criminal justice administration from Sam Houston State University (1982). He has served as a project director and principal member of several national police research initiatives funded by the National Institute of Justice, involving topics such as: fear reduction, organizational change, criminal investigations, cultural diversity, measuring what matters, and training. He has authored numerous department reports and articles for textbooks, magazines, and journals on various police management issues. Dr. Oettmeier has been the recipient of the Police Executive Research Forum's Gary P. Hayes Award in recognition of his outstanding initiative and commitment in furthering the improvement of the quality of police services.

Ken Peak is professor and former chair of the Department of Criminal Justice at the University of Nevada-Reno. He entered municipal policing in Kansas in 1970 and subsequently held positions as criminal justice planner; director of the Four-State Technical Assistance Institute, Law Enforcement Assistance Administration; director of university police, Pittsburg State

University; instructor at Washburn University; and assistant professor at Wichita State University. While at the University of Nevada-Reno he was named "Teacher of the Year" and also served as acting director of public safety. He has authored or coauthored 18 books, 16 of which are textbooks on general policing, community policing, justice administration, and police supervision and management, and two of which are historical books on bootlegging and temperance. He has also published more than 50 journal articles and book chapters on a wide range of justice-related subjects. He has served as chair of the Police Section of the Academy of Criminal Justice Sciences and president of the Western and Pacific Association of Criminal Justice Educators. He received two gubernatorial appointments to statewide criminal justice committees while in Kansas, and holds a doctorate from the University of Kansas.

Les Poole is an independent consultant with IMPACT Group, New York. He has a first degree in law from the University of Kent (1974) and a master of philosophy degree in policy analysis from the University of Exeter (1993). For 34 years he was with New Scotland Yard, London, and retired as a commander/assistant director of personnel for the Metropolitan Police Service. He was previously commander of operations for South West London and director of police training for England and Wales, and has served as a visiting professor at John Jay College of Criminal Justice. In 1994 he was awarded the Queen's Police Medal for services to British policing. Since retiring to the United States he has worked with the Police Foundation, International Association of Chiefs of Police, National Sheriff's Association, The Performance Institute, and the Southern Police Institute as a consultant and lecturer, and has carried out management audits and provided managerial and technical assistance to federal, state, and local police agencies across the United States. He has written a number of articles for *The Police Journal, Police Review,* and more recently for the Community Policing Consortium.

Jeff Rojek is an instructor in the Department of Sociology and Criminal Justice at Saint Louis University, and is currently completing his Ph.D. in criminology and criminal justice at the University of Missouri–St. Louis. He is a former officer with the Los Angeles Police Department and his research pursuits are in the area of officer and organization behavior in law enforcement. Some of his recent research efforts have included the organization and operations of police tactical units, the sustainability of innovation in problem-oriented policing efforts, analysis of traffic stops and the possibility of racial bias, and the function of temporary law enforcement organizations for security events. He has recently published articles in *Police Quarterly*.

D. Kim Rossmo is a research professor in the Department of Criminal Justice at Texas State University, and a management consultant with the Bureau of Alcohol, Tobacco, Firearms and Explosives. Formerly, he was the director of research for the Police Foundation, and the detective inspector in charge of the Vancouver Police Department's Geographic Profiling Section. Over the course of his 21-year policing career he worked assignments in organized crime intelligence, emergency response, patrol, crime prevention, and community liaison. He holds a Ph.D. (Simon Fraser University) in criminology and has researched and published in the areas of policing, offender profiling, and environmental criminology. Dr. Rossmo is a member of the International Association of Chiefs of Police Advisory Committee for Police Investigative Operations, the International Criminal Investigative Analysis Fellowship, and the South Carolina Research Authority Integrated Solutions Group Advisory Board. He is also an adjunct professor at Simon Fraser University and sits on the editorial board for the international journal *Homicide Studies*. He has recently studied stranger rape and geo-demographics in the United Kingdom and the geographic patterns associated with illegal land crossings along the southern U.S. border.

Steven Rutzebeck is director of the special investigations unit for GEICO Insurance. He is responsible for the administration of a countrywide insurance fraud investigative unit consisting of 250 investigators. In 1999 he retired as a captain with the Maryland State Police after 25 years of service. During one of his last assignments with the Maryland State Police he simultaneously held the positions of commander of professional development and associate director, Mid-Atlantic Regional Community Policing Institute at Johns Hopkins University. He also had the opportunity to serve as commander of the training division as well as commander of the crime prevention unit during his tenure with the state police. One of his major accomplishments involved coordinating the development of a national problem-based entrance-level training curriculum for law enforcement agencies. He is a nationally recognized educator on topics such as community policing, strategic planning, organizational change, time management, problem solving and facilitation. Rutzebeck holds a master's degree in legal studies from the University of Baltimore and a bachelor's degree from Pennsylvania State University.

Michael S. Scott is the director of the Center for Problem-Oriented Policing, Inc. and clinical assistant professor at the University of Wisconsin-Madison Law School. He was formerly chief of police in Lauderhill, Florida; served in various civilian administrative positions in the St. Louis Metropolitan, Ft. Pierce, Florida, and New York City police departments; and was a police officer in the Madison, Wisconsin, Police Department. Scott developed training programs in problem-oriented policing at the Police Executive Research Forum (PERF), and is a judge for PERF's Herman Goldstein Award for Excellence in Problem-Oriented Policing. He was the 1996 recipient of the Gary P. Hayes Award for innovation and leadership in policing. Scott holds a law degree from Harvard Law School and a bachelor's degree from the University of Wisconsin-Madison.

Quint Thurman is professor of criminal justice and department chair at Texas State University-San Marcos. He received a Ph.D. in sociology from the University of Massachusetts (Amherst) in 1987. His publications include four books and more than 30 refereed articles that have appeared in such journals as the *American Behavioral Scientist, Crime and Delinquency, Criminology and Public Policy, Social Science Quarterly, Public Finance, Justice Quarterly, Police Quarterly*, and the *Journal of Quantitative Criminology*. Books published in 2004 include a second edition of *Community Policing in a Rural Setting* (with co-author Edmund McGarrell) and an anthology, *Contemporary Policing: Controversies, Challenges, and Solutions* (with Jihong Zhao).

Index